Contemporary Bird Carvings

Two Generations of Bird Carvers

The Garfinkle Family Collection

Schiffer Publishing Ltd
4880 Lower Valley Road, Atglen, PA 19310 USA

In Memory of Sandor Garfinkle

Contemporary Bird Carvings

Two Generations of Bird Carvers

The Garfinkle Family Collection

An exhibition dedicated to the Brunet Family at the Ward Museum of Wildfowl Art, Salisbury University, Salisbury, Maryland

February 28 – June 25, 2006

Text by Kenneth Basile

Photographs courtesy of

Sandy Garfinkle and Kenneth Basile

the Ward Museum®
Salisbury University

Cover photo: Tan Brunet, "Wigeon Pair."
Frontispiece photo:Larry Barth. "Black-throated Green Warbler." 1986.
Back cover photo: Jett Brunet. "Mallard Pair," 1992.

Library of Congress Cataloging-in-Publication Data

Basile, Kenneth.
Contemporary bird carvings : two generations of bird carvers : the Garfinkle family collection : an exhibition dedicated to the Brunet family at the Ward Museum Of Wildfowl Art, Salisbury University, Salisbury, Maryland February 28-June 25, 2006 / text by Kenneth Basile ; photographs courtesy of Sandy Garfinkle and Kenneth Basile.
p. cm.
ISBN 0-7643-2501-9 (hardcover)
1. Wood-carving—United States—History—20th century—Exhibitions. 2. Decoys (Hunting)—United States—Exhibitions. 3. Garfinkel family—Art collections—Exhibitions. 4. Decoys (Hunting)—Private collections—United States—Exhibitions. I. Garfinkle, Sandy. II. Ward Museum Of Wildfowl Art (Salisbury, Md.) III. Title.

NK9712.B372 2006
745.593'6097307475225—dc22

2006004886

Designed by "Sue"
Type set in Zurich CnBT /New Baskerville BT

ISBN: 0-7643-2501-9
Printed in China

Published by Schiffer Publishing Ltd.
4880 Lower Valley Road
Atglen, PA 19310
Phone: (610) 593-1777; Fax: (610) 593-2002
E-mail: Info@schifferbooks.com

For the largest selection of fine reference books on this and related subjects, please visit our web site at **www.schifferbooks.com**
We are always looking for people to write books on new and related subjects. If you have an idea for a book please contact us at the above address.

This book may be purchased from the publisher.
Include $3.95 for shipping.
Please try your bookstore first.
You may write for a free catalog.

In Europe, Schiffer books are distributed by
Bushwood Books
6 Marksbury Ave.
Kew Gardens
Surrey TW9 4JF England
Phone: 44 (0) 20 8392-8585; Fax: 44 (0) 20 8392-9876
E-mail: info@bushwoodbooks.co.uk
Website: www.bushwoodbooks.co.uk
Free postage in the U.K., Europe; air mail at cost.

Contents

Preface

> "...heaven and earth never agreed better
> to frame a place for mans habitation..."
> Captain John Smith, 1612,
> describing the Chesapeake Bay region

The Garfinkle Family Collection, which is presented in this catalogue, resulted from the efforts and the vision of my parents, Sandy and Rani Garfinkle. For them, assembling this collection was a labor of love, and they came to admire both the artistry of the carvings and the artists who created them. The men and women whose works and lives are recorded in this catalogue are among the foremost American artists of the last century. My father passed away in January 2004, shortly after the arrangements had been made to donate the Garfinkle Family Collection to the Ward Museum of Wildfowl Art, Salisbury University, Salisbury, Maryland. He would have relished the opportunity to work with Ken Basile on this catalogue. We hope that you will enjoy these works as much as he did.

My father was passionate about many things. Above all, he was a lover of nature and of what he called the great American outdoors. He was also a lover of art and of fine craftsmanship. These passions were brought together in the waterfowl carvings and paintings that he collected. My father considered decorative decoy carving to be a uniquely American folk art form. Therefore, his patronage of this art form was a way to support American artists and to promote their work. He and my mother also enjoyed the friendship of the carvers and their families, and these friendships were a source of great joy.

The decorative carvings shown in these pages represented an artistic ideal to my father. The artists, as both carvers and painters, must be proficient in a variety of skills, and to him this enhanced the aesthetic value of their work. He was also attracted to decoy carving because it was an art form in which he felt he could assemble a collection of the greatest living artists of the day. It would have been his hope that this catalogue will introduce the magic of their artistry to a broader audience.

The quote above was often mentioned to me by my father. It captured for him both an homage to the natural beauty of the Chesapeake Bay as well as a hint of the splendor of that region before it had become prey to development. The Ward Museum of Wildfowl Art is a more recent addition to the wonders of the Chesapeake Bay area, and it is appropriate that my parents' collection will now be a permanent part of that.

–Steven Garfinkle
Bellingham, Washington
November 20, 2006

Introduction

In early January 2004, I received a telephone call from Mr. Sandy Garfinkle. He told me he and his family had decided to donate their collection of decorative bird carvings to the Ward Museum. I asked Mr. Garfinkle who had created the carvings in his collection and how many carvings would be in this gift. When he told me the number of pieces the family was donating and who the carvers were, I immediately told him I'd be right down.

Soon after I arrived, the Garfinkles led me to the bird carving collection in their Florida home. At once I knew I was looking at something very important. Within the first hour, it was as if Sandy and I had known each other for a very long time. We spoke the language of the birds.

What incredible bird carvings they are. Among the 91 pieces, the collection includes nine hard-to-find decoys and four paintings by Larry Hayden. There are three birds of prey by Greg Woodard, one of the best sculptors of hawks and falcons working today. A heron by Gary Yoder, four pieces by Larry Barth, seven decorative decoys by Mike Bonner, two decorative decoys by Jude Brunet, and ten carvings by Jett Brunet are all part of this collection. The collection includes twenty-two decorative decoys by Tan Brunet, making the Ward Museum's collection of Brunet family carvings the largest. There are two decoys by Jim Foote. Pat Godin is represented by six of his decorative decoys, and there are four decoys by Pat's father-in-law, Jimmie Vizier. Bob Guge has four carvings in the collection. Ernie Muehlmatt is represented by one of his woodcocks. John Scheeler has an early redhead drake and a black duck in the collection. Also included are a ruffed grouse by Barbara Nelson, and a harlequin drake by Marc Schultz. Todd Wohlt and Rick Johannsen have pintail hens and John Gewerth has a blue-winged teal pair in the collection.

The Garfinkles donated the carvings and paintings to the Ward Museum along with all of the letters, catalogues, and other documents associated with acquiring the works of art. All of the artists represented in the collection have won in some class of the Ward World Championship Wildfowl Carving Competition. These are some of the most important bird artists working today and also in the history of contemporary bird carving.

In making this gift to the Ward Museum, Sandy Garfinkle requested that the museum produce this record of the collection and that a special reception be held to present the collection to the public. This catalogue is the product of his request. The reception was held on the 30th anniversary of the Ward Museum of Wildfowl Art, Salisbury University on June 10, 2006

Two generations of Cajun carvers. Jimmie Vizier, Jett Brunet, Tan Brunet, 1972.

When I began work on this catalogue I realized, in order to understand better who these artists are and why they are making and presenting their art the way they do, I had to provide some context or background information. In 1982 I wrote a catalogue for an exhibition showing the historical movement of the decoy maker in the direction of decorative bird carving, titled *American Decorative Bird Carving, From Decoy to Decorative*. I have included material from this catalogue in the first section.

I have looked at this art form from a generational perspective. In evaluating the bird carvers working since the late 1800s through the 1900s, I found I was able to separate them into four distinct groups. All of these groups or generations of bird carvers participated in carving contests.

The first group was made up of decoy makers working throughout the nineteenth century and into the first two decades of the twentieth century. These included Lothrop Holmes, Benjamin Holmes, and Obadiah Verity.

The second generation consisted of decoy makers who, for the most part, were also involved in making decorative bird carvings. They worked in the early twentieth century, and included the Ward Brothers, Elmer Crowell, and Shang Wheeler.

The third generation, while still having some relationship with decoy carving, includes primarily decorative bird carvers.

The next generation includes the children of some of these carvers, as well as others in their age group, and can be generally defined by experimentation and attempts to take the art form to new, more interpretive levels. While the fourth generation of decorative bird carvers still actively participate in bird carving competitions and the decoy traditions that form the basis of many of these contests, their focus is not primarily on the floating duck, but on all wildfowl.

Artists in the third or fourth generation can be distinguished from their predecessors by the tools they use. Today artists work with woodburning tools, mechanical grinders, acrylic paints, resins, bird skins, live captive birds, and photography. They deal with the concepts of negative and positive space, mass and density. They understand how the eye works and how we perceive the world around us.

Many of the younger artists in the Garfinkle Family Collection are trained artists or biologists, but all four generations of bird carvers know how a bird works and how it fits into its natural world. This catalogue is the story of the third and fourth generations of American bird carvers.

Because of the nature of the Garfinkle Family Collection it is not possible to include all of the outstanding decorative bird carvers working during the last twenty-five years of the 20th century, though the Garfinkles did acquire works by most of the important bird artists working during this time.

Bird Carving Exhibitions & Contests: 1876-2000

People have been evaluating bird carvings in formal carving competitions since 1876. The first two generations of carvers made decoys that were created primarily to catch birds, even if they were sometimes decorative in style. But throughout the twentieth and into the twenty-first centuries, the bird carving contest played an increasingly important role in the working life of bird carvers. The third and fourth generations of carvers were encouraged and largely directed by carving shows and competitions. The decoys and decorative bird carvings by these later carvers were made primarily for sale to collectors. The Garfinkle collection represents the best of the third and fourth generations of carvers in this uniquely American art form.

This is a story of carving competitions and the effects these competitions had on creativity and the forward visual movement of an art form, from the decoy to decorative bird carving. Within the past century, the American art form of carving wildfowl in wood has gone through a major transition. Until the early 1900s, the wildfowl carver concentrated on decoys for hunting. By the late 1960s, the art form had turned almost exclusively to decorative carvings admired for their realistic beauty.

During the transitional period many forces were responsible for the change in the carver's objective. In the early twentieth century, laws were established to stop commercial hunting, or market gunning, because the once large flocks of waterfowl were declining. The professional bird hunter and decoy maker turned to other sources to make a living. Many of these men became professional guides for recreational hunters. What started as a conservation measure effectively stopped a major industry.

It also led to the promotion of a new American art form. In the years that followed, exhibitions of bird carvings were held to make the public more aware of the country's great wildfowl resources. These shows and contests introduced the public to beautiful bird carvings, created a market for the bird carver, and advanced an art form unique to the American experience.

But recognition of the humble decoy as an art form was long in coming. When evaluating decoys in the late 19th and early 20th centuries, most people looked at the maker's technical skills rather than his artistic vision. Bird carvings were judged on floating characteristics, construction techniques, quality of paint work, and the ability to bring a bird within range of the gunner. This method of evaluating bird carvings continued, in later years, to have a profound effect upon the art form.

The first known gathering and evaluation of decoys was held as a small part of the International Centennial Exposition in Philadelphia in 1876. The U.S. Animal Resources and Fisheries

Department's exhibit included swimming decoys made from skins, wood decoy waders, decoy swimming birds in wood and tin, and wood decoys, among others. Benjamin Holmes, a carver from Stratford, Connecticut, was awarded a gold medal for his twelve bluebills or greater scaup decoys. His work was probably exhibited by Frances Burritt, who collected his decoys. [Freshour, interview]

The first real decoy show was held in 1923 at Bellport, Long Island. This novel event was put on by the Howell's Point Anti-Duskers Society. Dusking refers to the shooting of ducks in their feeding areas at twilight. Formed by sportsmen who loved to hunt legally, the Society's sole purpose was to draw attention to and stop illegal dusk hunting. They sponsored the 1923 Bellport show, the only show the society ever produced. However, this show started a trend of collecting and showing decoys which was to skyrocket after World War II. This contest drew about 200 decoys, some "finished off in marvelous detail and the grace of their shapes and poise would do credit to a classic style sculptor, while others are rather impressionistic in finish..." ["Novel Decoy Exhibit Held at Bellport," p. 1]

Decoy carvers/hunters of the Great South Bay, New York, area painted their hunting decoys quickly and easily with solid colors, except for the heads of black duck decoys, which they

Benjamin Holmes. "Bluebill Drake," 1876. Holmes won the first decoy contest, held at the Philadelphia Centennial, with twelve bluebill decoys. Sorenson Collection, Ward Museum of Wildfowl Art.

painted with feather detail. It was considered too much work and not necessary to paint feathers on the black duck bodies. When these locals entered their decoys in the 1923 contest they thoroughly expected to be winners, but they had a shock coming to them when they saw "Shang" Wheeler's decoys, which were carved and painted to look like live birds. Wheeler had been influenced by his Stratford, Connecticut, predecessors, including classic, first generation carvers like Albert Lang and Benjamin Holmes. The Bellport contest, in fact, marked the transition from the first generation of bird carvers to the second generation. Because Wheeler's carvings were not from gunning rigs, as were many of the other entries, they were considered impractical by the seasoned hunter. In later years, practicality was one of the criteria for judging decoys.

Elmer Crowell, also a contestant, was given recognition for his shorebird carvings. Another variation from the gunning rig theme was an exhibit of miniature decoys by John H. B. Boyle. Joel Barber, the author of the first book about decoys and acclaimed father of decoy collecting, was a prime force behind later shows and also exhibited and competed in this contest.

The duck show idea, started on Long Island with great success, was not repeated there until 1964, forty-one years later. However, in 1924, the Second Annual Exhibition of Wild-Fowl Decoys by American Sportsmen was held at the Winchester Sportsmen's Headquarters in New York City. The committee was made up of many of the same people who organized the 1923 Long Island show. Its stated purpose was to further the work of the Bellport exhibition and to encourage the current revival of decoy making by sportsmen. The judging was based on the practical use and maintenance of decoys. Samuel Barnes of Havre de Grace, Maryland, won Best in Show with a pair of canvasback decoys. The categories in the contest were simply "Hand-made Decoys" and "Machine-made Decoys," though the latter were not eligible for prizes.

It was too early to even consider decorative carving in competition. However, miniatures, the forerunners of today's decorative carvings, were again exhibited at this 1924 show. John Lee Baldwin is listed in the program as having exhibited miniature flying birds and decoys.

According to Joel Barber, after the 1924 show the "interest subsided, to revive again in an 'Exhibition of Wild Fowl Decoys,' held in New York in the fall of 1931." That same fall, in November, the Newark Museum sponsored an exhibit of "so-called American Folk Sculpture and included among the exhibits a group of old decoys." [Barber, p. 9] Then follows a lapse of information until 1941, when the National Sportsmen's Show was held in New York City, but again there is little known about the event. Possibly World War II caused the duck shows to shut down.

In 1947 and 1948 the National Decoy Makers Contest and Exhibition was held at Grand Central Palace, New York City, sponsored by R. J. Schaefer of Schaefer Brewing Company. There were no categories in the contest for decorative carvings. In the 1948 show, Lem Ward won several awards for his decoys, including Best Decoy in Show, Best Diving Duck Decoy, and Best Professional Hand-made Decoy; however, he has said he was not allowed to enter his decorative carvings in the contest. [Ward, interview]

Lem Ward's "Sleeping Mallard Drake" won Best of Show at the National Decoy Makers Contest held in New York City in 1948. Ward was not allowed to enter his decorative carvings in this contest though his winning decoy verges on formal sculpture. Collection of W. H. Purnell, Jr., and Kaye Purnell.

In 1949, the name of the New York City show was changed to the International Decoy Makers Contest and Exhibition, and a new category, Best Ornamental Decoy, was added. This was won by Harry Ross's (Old Saybrook, Connecticut) ruddy duck and was probably the first award for a decorative in the history of duck shows.

The contest, which had come to be referred to as the "Nationals," was discontinued after 1951. Not until 1960, through the efforts of Bob Birchler, who wanted a place to show his carvings, was the National Decoy Contest reborn as part of a sportsmen's show in Syracuse, New York. It was opened to amateurs only and drew over 200 entrants. The following year it was open to both amateurs and professionals. Writing in 1963, Birchler stated that, "The coming of plastic decoys and the decline in waterfowl has discouraged great numbers of gunners from making decoys. And while the National contest may not have stirred interest in mak-

National Decoy Contest, Syracuse, New York, March 8, 1964. Left to right: Ralph Loeff, H. B. Evans, Joel Barber, William Mackey, Bob Birchler. Photo by Frank Cardinali. Sorenson Collection, Ward Museum of Wildfowl Art.

ing gunning decoys, it has encouraged many sportsmen to take a crack at making decorative decoys. It seems almost every duck hunter and bird fancier has a decoy of some sort or another used as a home decoration." [Birchler, pp. 7-8]

In 1964, the Great South Bay Waterfowlers Association, Inc., held the first decoy contest on Long Island since the premier show of 1923. Held at Babylon, Long Island, it has been an annual event ever since. [Wyatt, p. 24] In 1965, the Davenport, Iowa, show was started. Also that year the Canadian National Sportsmen's show was held in Toronto with 115 decoys entered. [Sorenson, p. 10]

Until this time shows had usually been a combination of contests and exhibitions. Then, in 1965, the Kent County Chapter of the Maryland Ornithological Society held a true exhibition of wildfowl carvings at Chestertown, Maryland. This was so well attended and appreciated that another was held in 1967, drawing such crowds that the facilities couldn't accommodate them. [Sorenson, p. 111] This inspired a group of Eastern Shore of Maryland carvers and businessmen to hold a larger exhibit in the spacious Wicomico County Youth and Civic Center at Salisbury, Maryland, a central location on the shore. They named their organization The Ward Foundation in honor of Lem and Steve Ward, pioneers in decorative bird carving, and held their first Wildfowl Carving and Art Exhibition in the fall of 1968.

Though there is evidence of decoratives being judged in contests as early as 1949, their place in the decoy contest had not been clearly established even in the mid-1960s. Judges at that time were unsure of how to establish criteria for judging decoratives and how much decorative touch should be allowed. In 1965, Ralph M. Loeff explained:

> With decoy shows popping up in more and more areas, a collector's chances of being asked to serve as a judge became increasingly probable. It happened to me when the Great Mississippi Valley Fair, Davenport, Iowa, sponsored the first national decoy contest ever to be held in the Midwest. I was asked to judge decorative waterfowl – note the term "waterfowl" rather than decoy – and accepted without too much thought. The contest, incidentally, had two sets of judges, three judges for gunning decoys and three judges for decorative waterfowl. I believe that in past decoy contests, the same judges were used for both gunning and decorative classes. As the date of the contest came closer, it occurred to me and my fellow judges, Harold Haertel and Hal Sorenson that we would have to decide what constituted a winner from a loser.

How does one judge the "best" decorative waterfowl?

First, we decided that a decorative waterfowl certainly does not have to be a decoy. It is strictly a carving or sculpture produced by the artist as a piece of art to be displayed in a home, museum, etc. With that fact established, we turned our attention to establishing some standards.

We decided that the same standards which apply to any art show should be applied to decorative waterfowl. Composition, content, form, and color were the factors we had to consider. This meant that a carving that was simple but beautifully conceived could beat out an elaborately detailed piece with every feather carved and painted. It meant, too, that a fine primitive or nonrepresentational piece could compete on equal terms with a sophisticated lifelike carving. After all, Grandma Moses and Picasso hang in museums along with Rembrandt and El Greco.

In the show that we judged, all of the carvings were representational, emulating the actual birds as closely as possible. This eliminated the possibility of a primitive winning "best of show" – there just weren't any. The trend in recent decorative entries has been for unusual bird poses such as spread wings, open bills, etc. These birds could hardly be considered decoys; hence, the use of the term decorative waterfowl. In the Great Mississippi Valley Fair contest, there were many fine entries and we had a difficult time picking the first three or even the first five. [Loeff, pp. 10-11]

Gunning decoys had been judged on their correctness in every detail in duplicating the live bird – plumage patterns, color, construction and stability on water. In 1965, William J. Mackey, Jr., a judge of gunning decoys since 1948, said, "My chief concern is a tendency for expert carvers to 'guss up' decoys until they are really ornamentals rather than working 'stools.' It is a fad that can be carried too far. Also of concern is entry of exhibits that are one of a kind on which so much time has been spent that no one could possibly make a rig of them. Perhaps only entries of which at least a half dozen have been made would tend to solve the problem. On the other hand, perhaps the striving for single decoy excellence is a good thing." [Mackey, p. 9]

There was an uncertainty as to what to do about decorative carvings, where to draw the line between the practical and the artistic, or whether to draw a line at all.

A year later, 1966, another veteran judge, Harold Sorenson, was expressing problems in setting up entries and standards for judging. One of the concerns of the time was that gunning class decoys were becoming too decorative. Some makers were carving strictly for contests and it was judged unfair that they be allowed to compete against those who carved whole rigs of working decoys. [Sorenson, p. 26]

Robert Kerr of Smith Falls, Ontario, also carved and competed with both decoys and decoratives. According to Harold Sorenson in a 1965 *Decoy Collector's Guide*, "His hunting decoys, like his decorative birds, are quite detailed both in carving and painting. In fact, I asked Bob, 'Just what is the difference between your working decoys and the ones you carve for the mantel?' Bob thought a minute and then replied, 'I guess you could say I put a keel on the gunning decoys and put a felt cloth on the bottom of the decorative models.'" [Sorenson, p. 26]

Bird carvers and the people who organized the carving contests from the 1920s through the 1960s were trying to come to terms with the two directions, functional bird decoys and decorative bird carvings. The emphasis was no longer on the abstract qualities attained by the decoy maker. By the early 1960s, it was economically unjustifiable for the sportsman hunter to purchase handmade wooden decoys. The handmade decoy business for

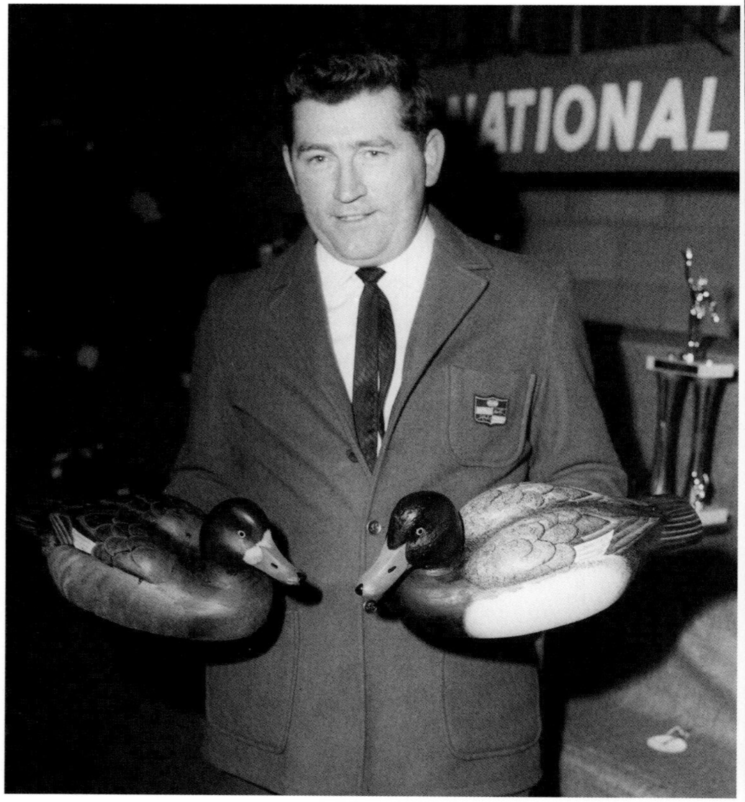

Robert Kerr holding two of his decoys at the 1964 National Decoy Contest in Syracuse, New York. When asked the difference between his working decoys and the ones he made for the mantel he replied, "I put a keel on the gunning decoys and put a felt cloth on the bottom of the decorative models." Photo by Frank Cardinali. Sorenson Collection, Ward Museum of Wildfowl Art.

all practical purposes was a thing of the past. Machine made wooden decoys and plastic decoys had effectively eliminated the individual decoy maker.

But there was a marketplace for bird carvings. Hunting and the out-of-doors were too deeply a part of the American lifestyle. The door was opened for the art form to grow and mature. As early as the 1930s, carvers like the Ward Brothers Elmer Crowell, and Ira Hudson, the second generation of American bird carvers, were experimenting with birds in flight and putting legs and feathers on their decoys. By the 1960s, the works of these pioneers became tremendously important to bird carvers. Following in the stylistic footsteps of their predecessors, these carvers produced bird carvings that were solidly formed, but rather stylized in appearance, with paint patterns that were impressionistic, more in the tradition of the decoy maker than of today's bird carver.

Carvers like the Ward brothers and Ira Hudson were going in their own directions, creating bird carvings that reflected their own responses to their environments. In many cases different anatomical parts of the birds were not accurate. The paint work still maintained an individualism that had been developed over many years of carving decoys.

Lem Ward. "Green-winged Teal," 1940. Lem Ward was a pioneer in the use of feathering and experimental poses in his bird carvings. Lem Ward began working with feather inserts as early as 1940.

By 1968, carving took a new direction. The Rev. Jack Drake came up with the technique of feathering or making separate feathers to add to the realism of the total bird. Though the Ward Brothers had developed this technique in the 1930s, it was not until the middle to late 1960s that it was refined and expanded to produce more than just an impressionistic presentation of the quality of feathers. [Basile, p 42]

The bird carving world quickly picked up this idea of creating extreme realism through the fragmentation, or carving parts and applying them to a body. Some carvers went to the extent of replicating the exact number of feathers on the real bird and attaching them to the carved body. The realism achieved through the use of such specialized tools as woodburners, homemade knives and gauges, and some filler putty led to the creation of a carved bird that is virtually impossible to tell from a real bird. The emphasis was on the techniques used, the coloration, and the pose.

In the late 1960s, the work of Gilbert Maggioni enabled wildfowl carving to make a visual quantum leap. Academically trained as an artist, Maggioni brought to the carving world such visual concepts as negative and positive space and an understanding of the complex interrelationships of the many parts to the whole. For the first time the environment became an important part of the sculpture. No longer was the bird isolated from its natural surroundings. The birds were part of a greater whole, sometimes being completely overwhelmed by their environment. Whole marshes or water scenes were constructed using not only wood, but resin, glass, wire, and bronze. The birds appeared to be suspended or actually flying through the air. No longer was the emphasis placed upon the maker's carving and painting ability, but upon his organization of the total composition. If this were not present the sculptures would not work.

Maggioni's emphasis was on the environment that he had constructed around the carvings. His birds in many cases blended

Gilbert Maggioni. "Dusting Bobwhite Quail," 1974.

into their surroundings. As in nature, they were controlled by their environment, totally dependent upon it. The natural color of the plumage and the bird's method of movement through the air in many cases made it difficult to distinguish the bird from the world around it.

Grainger McKoy, Maggioni's colleague, has followed his style, and has carried this concept even further, adding the dynamics of motion and force.

In 1971, the Ward Foundation began holding its World Champion Wildfowl Carving Competition in Salisbury, Maryland. It is interesting to note the effect this contest has had on the world of decorative bird carving. The competition has two main classes. The Decorative Decoy class still supports the traditional concept of the decoy. The winner of the first year's competition, John Garton, won with a pair of teal that, for all practical purposes, could be used as decoys. But from 1972, with John Scheeler's winning red breasted mergansers, the work became technically more and more complex. With highly detailed carving and feathering, the only resemblance these carvings had to the old decoys was the fact that they floated. But the basis and premise of the carvings remained in the tradition of the decoy.

Grainger McKoy. "Green-winged Teal," 1981.

Tan Brunet, of Galliano, Louisiana, who won this competition three times, added a new dimension to the presentation of his birds. His ducks were placed on a piece of driftwood, which was attached to a highly finished and shaped piece of mahogany. This was a radical departure from any method of presentation that had been entered into any carving contest up until this time. Even more important than the use of driftwood as a stand was Tan's addition of two miniature carved flying canvasbacks attached to the driftwood just below the main subject. Brunet had borrowed the idea of the remarque from the wildfowl printmakers and added a three dimensional remarque to his piece.

The other part of the Ward Foundation's Wildfowl Carving Competition is the Lifesize Decorative category. This category, unlike the early contests, is directed toward the creation of lifesize wildfowl. The emphasis is not upon the carving of floating waterfowl, but on the creation of any kind of bird in its natural setting. The main focus of these carvings is on the spectacular birds themselves. The carving contest has become a major proving ground for up-and-coming carvers of this genre.

With the encouragement of carving contests held throughout the United States and Canada, the third and fourth generations of bird carvers have evolved. The carvers represented by the Garfinkle collection are an excellent grouping of artists who have had the carving shows and competitions as forums where they could develop their visual ideas, using the bird as their expressive vehicle and riding it into the 21st century.

Two Generations of Bird Carvers

James Foote (1925-2004)

With an academic background in forestry and wildlife management, Jim Foote spent twenty-seven years working for the Michigan Department of Natural Resources in Atlanta, Michigan, and the Point Mouille State Game Area in Rockwood, Michigan. Foote came from a family of physicians, but at an early age decided he preferred to study and work with nature. After serving in World War II, he attended the University of Michigan.

As a young boy Foote began carving decoys because of his involvement in fishing and hunting. It was not until his forties that he became seriously involved with professional bird carving and started entering bird carving contests held in the Midwest, Canada, and the East Coast. He won many decoy contest prizes during the 1970s, including the Ward Foundation's World Championship Wildfowl Carving Competition Decorative Decoy Pairs in 1973 and 1975.

Foote was a self-trained artist, developing many of the techniques he used in making his decorative decoys. Tan Brunet, who won the World Championship in 1976, said of him, "His work was loose and had character." [Brunet, interview] Foote felt that many competitive carvers had achieved such a good level of technical competence that their decoys were beginning to all look alike. Rejecting this trend toward carvers as technicians, Foote "...wanted to see more individualistic carvers, like a Tan Brunet." [Crandell, p. 4]

By the end of the mid 1970s he had quit his work as a natural resources biologist to devote all of his time to wildlife art. He continued entering decoy contests until the late 1970s. In 1977 he decided he wanted to be a painter of wildlife scenes and produce limited edition prints of his paintings. He stopped entering carvings in carving contests, though he did continue volunteering as a judge in many contests.

Jim Foote was one of the first professional carvers to actually add feather texturing to carvings that are essentially traditional decoys. While making ducks that work like decoys, he gave a sense of animation and realism to his carvings that few professional carvers working prior to the early 1970s had achieved. He was an important influence on many of the more successful carvers working during the next ten years.

By the late 1980s Foote was also carving fish decoys and was one of the founders in 1989 of the Great Lakes Fish Decoy Collectors & Carvers Association. His fish and bird decoys are sought by many collectors of wildlife art.

Left: James Foote. "Green-winged Teal Pair," 1977 (10 1/4" x 41/2" x 4" each)

John Scheeler (1925-1987)

Many people considered John Scheeler a quiet, shy, and secretive person. He didn't have to say much about what he was doing because he felt his work said it all. Scheeler, from Mays Landing, New Jersey, is recognized as one of the most important bird carvers of the later 20th century. He made his reputation by entering his bird carvings in contests all around the United States. At the Ward Foundation's World Championship Wildfowl Carving Competition, he won the World Championship Decorative Lifesize competition seven times and in other contests he captured over 200 First and Best of Show awards.

Scheeler didn't begin competing until he was forty-three. As a young boy, he made a few decoys but didn't really become serious until 1969, when he visited the Ward Foundation's annual Carving and Art Exhibition held in Salisbury, Maryland. As a young man he was interested in studying painting as a way to improve the realism of his early decoys. He took a correspondence course from the Famous Artists School. He said he paid $500 for the course but had to drop out when his daughters got sick. [Schroeder, p. 169] When he went to the Ward Foundation's annual show, he liked what he saw and decided he was going to start making birds for competitions. Scheeler said he "walked in the door; it nearly blew me away." [Schroeder p. 170]

Left: John Scheeler. "Redhead Drake," 1971 (11 3/4" x 61/2" x 71/2")

In 1971, he entered his first carving contest at the U.S. Open held in Babylon, New York. He won Best in Show. In 1972, he won the Best in World Decorative Decoy Pairs at the World Championship Wildfowl Carving Competition. The redhead decoy he carved in 1971 is one of the first carvings made by Scheeler. It shows the great natural talent this artist brought to

John Scheeler. Detail of paint on "Redhead Drake," 1971

the art form. At this early date in his carving career, he already had an understanding of bird anatomy. Ken Scheeler, John's brother, said, "He told me that a lot of carvers did neater work than he did and that he just couldn't come up with super clean birds. But if you stepped back a few feet, they had the look that many of those carvers couldn't capture." [Schroeder, p. 90] Scheeler was an impressionistic painter. By placing dabs of paint on the bird in such a way as brought the image together, he was able to paint with a style that gave the impression of great realism. Ken Scheeler commented, "John contributed a lot in terms of design and composition, but his special contribution was the look of the birds. I think they were in a class by themselves because of that. A lot of carvers would make birds that looked more like decoys than birds. But John would put in lumps and bumps to bring out the character." [Schroeder, p. 91] The decoy carver Larry Hayden added, "I look at John's work as sculpture. His methods were so different from the way I carve: I use tight patterns, but his works came as much from his mind and hands as they did from patterns." [Schroeder, p. 97] It was evident from a very early stage in his career that he was a great artist.

Prior to 1973, he worked as an industrial painter. After winning the 1973 World Championship Lifesize Class, he changed his profession from painter to wildlife sculptor. Scheeler began to work exclusively on commission for Douglas Miller, a serious

Left: John Scheeler. "Black Duck," 1985 (16" x 7" x 5 3/4")

wildlife art collector from Colorado. Miller was a patron to many bird artists and supported a number of them full-time. Scheeler was very fortunate; being able to make whatever he wanted led to an unusual freedom to grow as an artist. He now had the time to devote to his artistic ideas, without the pressure of worrying about selling his work.

The fact that he had been a consistent winner of the carving world's most prestigious competition is secondary to the impact he continues to have on the history of the art form. Scheeler is known as an innovator in both his carving techniques and the visual content of his carvings. Early in his career he became known as an expert decorative decoy carver and later for his aggressive birds of prey, often just completing a kill. Just as complex in concept and organization, though, are his carvings of grouse, surf scoters, clapper rails, and terns. In these works he is a master of understatement, showing subtle relationships between color, form and an environment that, while appearing natural, are very carefully thought out. A life force runs through his work that very few carvers have been able to achieve.

Scheeler made one to two carvings a year. He was a master at feather insertion but did not feel that it was essential to carve and insert every individual feather. He preferred to use or develop new techniques that allowed him to create the visual impression for which he was striving. He worked an eight-hour day, five days a week. When he first started carving in the late sixties, he put in as many as fourteen hours a day, seven days a week, but found that he became more productive when he regulated his time and gave himself a break. [Schroeder, p. 91]

Scheeler used many different methods to prepare for the final construction of his carving. Many times he'd skin a bird to see the relationship of the feathers to the underlying body structure. Often he used the actual body for his pattern. He noted that taxidermists made rubber molds of bird bodies to be used in mounts. These molds, Scheeler felt, were helpful to him in his work. One of his biggest problems was the structure and location of the bird's legs. Sometimes he would work in clay to set up the composition of a piece, but usually he planned it all in his imagination.

While very much a realist, he didn't let realism get in the way of his artistic sense or vision, but used the reality of nature as a tool to achieve his ultimate end. He liked his pieces stylized. He arranged his bird in an artistic, not necessarily typical pose, but made sure his bird's proportions were correct.

"When you put a lot of modeling in a bird, you can't finish it right down to the last detail. Instead you have to create an illusion. There is a lot more to the bird than the final finish," he continued. "You can't put the icing on the cake until you make the cake." [Basile, p. 27] To Scheeler, balance was of the utmost importance; without proper balance in the whole piece, it won't work.

John Scheeler died in 1987, leaving behind a legacy that carvers today view as the standard for which they strive.

Ernest Muehlmatt (1927–)

Ernie Muehlmatt has always been involved with art. He grew up in Springfield, Pennsylvania, a suburb of Philadelphia. His father was a Swiss immigrant, coming to this country in the early 20th century. His mother came from a German background. By the time he was born, in 1927, his parents had set up a florist business, wholesaling and retailing flowers and flower arrangements. Muehlmatt and his brother were to stay in this business until they were in their early forties.

Besides learning the finer aspects of flower arranging Muehlmatt always liked to draw. Arranging flowers taught him three-dimensional design. After serving in World War II, Muehlmatt enrolled in the Philadelphia College of Art on the GI Bill. After a year he transferred to the Philadelphia Art Student League and studied four more years, graduating with a diploma in advertising art.

After finishing his art training he went back into the family flower business. For the next twenty years he painted children's portraits and arranged flowers for weddings. Because of the wedding business, he is a bird carver today. One day in 1968, when he was around forty, he received a call from a wedding party asking him where the flowers were. He realized he had gotten the date wrong, but within a matter of hours he and his brother put together the flower order. After this he and his brother, tired of the stresses of the job, shut down the flower business.

Muelhmatt continued running a garden center which had been part of the flower business. As part of the garden center he added a bird shop, selling anything that had to do with wild birds, including bird houses, seed, bird books, and bird baths. During this time he met Robert Hogue, who was a bird carver, and it was Hogue who got Muehlmatt into carving birds. Muehlmatt started by carving chickadees to sell in his bird shop. At first he could produce ten chickadees a day, but with experience he began producing more chickadees than he could sell in his garden center. He then started wholesaling his little birds for $6.00 each to gift shops at the New Jersey shore. He found he had the beginnings of a lucrative small business selling his carved birds.

In 1969 he read an article about the Ward Foundation's Wildfowl Carving and Art Exhibition held in Salisbury, Maryland. Muehlmatt, like his future friend and fellow bird carver, John Scheeler, didn't know any other bird carvers. Through the activities of the Ward Foundation, which had been set up to promote the art form of bird carving, they received their first introduction to bird carving . Muehlmatt visited the show and met his old friend Bob Dunn, who was also from the Philadelphia

Left: Ernest Muehlmatt. "Woodcock," 1986 (11" x 11" x 10")

area. Dunn was the chairman of the exhibition. In 1970 Muelhmatt was invited to show his bird carvings at the Salisbury show. He sold all of the carvings he had on display and realized that he could support himself and his family being a sculptor of birds. He went back to Springfield and sold the family business.

For many years Ernie Muehlmatt only participated in activities sponsored by the Ward Foundation and the Easton Waterfowl Festival which is held in Easton, Maryland, every November. During the 1970s and 1980s he became one of the most successful bird carvers working. Business was good. By the 1990s Muelhmatt had won the Ward Foundation World Championship Decorative Lifesize and Miniature Competitions several times. He had also won numerous Best of Show awards at other carving contests. But the business of bird carving began to change. His work during the 1990s and into the 21st century became centered more on giving carving seminars and selling more inexpensive reproductions of his bird carvings.

When he first started making carved birds his focus was on painting. He stayed away from woodburning or the actual carving of feathers. He felt the use of woodburning tools was for people who could not paint. Then, in the early 1980s he first met the World Champion decoy carver, Tan Brunet, while displaying his carvings at the Easton Waterfowl Festival. Brunet, a master carver from Louisiana, was displaying a pintail hen that had been burned, but, because Brunet had not had the time, was not painted. When Ernie Muehlmatt saw it on display, he was impressed with the way Tan Brunet was able to change the coloration of the bird's feathers by varying the temperature of his woodburning tool. Using the burner alone Brunet was even able to create shadows, shading, and a feeling of softness in the bird's feathers. This new development had the bird carving world seriously looking at the potential of woodburning. Everyone who saw Brunet's pintail told him not to paint the decoy, but to leave it like it was.

Muelhmatt was quite impressed with Brunet's work, and when he returned to his studio he undertook carving using no paint. He now wanted to focus on woodburning instead of emphasizing painting in his carvings. His first carving using only woodburning for coloration was a miniature great horned owl. He displayed this piece at a carving exhibition sponsored by the Eastman Kodak Company in New York City. Muelhmatt said, "It was a show stopper and I immediately sold the owl." [Muelhmatt, interview] From this time on he decided he wanted to burn for color whenever he could. He used the burning pen like a brush, applying transparent color washes over the burning. The woodcock he made in 1986, purchased by the Garfinkle family, is an excellent example of this approach to coloring and feather sculpting.

The addition of burning techniques to his developing skill as a bird carver also acted as a catalyst for more changes in his style. His carvings give a sense of the underlying musculature of the bird. He now tries to accentuate different aspects of his works. In his carving Muelhmatt likes to highlight what he feels are the more important aspects of his bird sculpture leaving what is less important visually played down. "It is the overall effect that is important. It is no longer a matter of making an exact reproduction of a bird." [Muelhmatt, interview]

While he still uses the bird carving contest as a vehicle to show his work and gain recognition for it, he would like to have a juried exhibition with no rules. He would like to see an event that encourages the artist to express himself outside of any required structured presentation. Muehlmatt does not like rules. This is evident in the way he lives and the way he makes his art. "The art of making a bird is just one way for the artist to express his ideas about the world around him. The bird carver should be rewarded for this." [Muelhmatt, interview]

Jimmie Vizier (1933–)

The Vizier family moved to the southern bayous of Louisiana from Canada in the 1800s. They were trappers, fishermen, and hunters and settled in an area of Bayou LaFourche known as Caminada Village on Grand Isle. Beauregard Vizier lived there with his wife and ten children. Three of his children, Clovis, Beauregard and Odee are recognized as master decoy makers, having made thousands of decoys in their lifetimes. Jimmie is one of Odee's two sons. His brother, Tom, also carved, though in a more contemporary style.

Before it became hard to find, most decoy makers in Louisiana used cypress root as their primary material. Having no power tools, they worked with hatchets and knives. The wood was soft, easy to carve, light and easy to handle. Their decoys had to be made quickly and efficiently because frequently their birds were washed away in storms that frequented the Louisiana coast. Today most Louisiana decoy makers work with tupelo gum.

Vizier's father had a fishing camp where they would work, shrimping in the summer and oystering in the winter. When shrimping and oystering were out of season, they hunted birds. Vizier was hunting birds for the family from a very early age. By the time he was in the sixth grade, he left school and went to work hunting and fishing.

Vizier has carved birds since he was five. He says "Carving decoys is in my blood." [Vizier, interview] He had some of the best teachers living in the area, his father and uncle. Their influence on the carving traditions of Louisiana has been great.

Vizier is five years older than Tan Brunet, who is recognized as one of the most important contemporary decoy makers. Vizier grew up living next door to the Brunets in Galliano, Louisiana. Tan Brunet says, "He was my teacher. He started when he was a young boy carving alongside his daddy. He's a super talent. He has more talent than all of us as far as gunning birds. Jimmy was a big influence on me." [Badger, p. 26]

Left: Jimmie Vizier. "Mallard Drake," 1988 (18" x 7" x 8 3/4")

While he had a reputation as a master decoy maker from an early age, by the time he was 19 he had entered the Marine Corps and found himself fighting in Korea for three years. His Marine Corps experiences never left him. After separation from the military he moved back to Galliano and began work on tugboats in the area. In his mid-thirties he and his brother started their own ocean-going tugboat business. Vizier had his captain's license and for the next 20 years they ran a fleet of tugs working with the oil rigs in the North Sea. Vizier relocated the family to London for several years.

He started to enter bird carving contests in 1971 in New Orleans. Also in 1971 the Viziers began traveling to the Ward Foundation's World Championship Wildfowl Carving Competition held in Salisbury, Maryland, in the spring and to the Easton Waterfowl Festival in Easton, Maryland, in the fall to show his carvings and to enter the competition. Since that time he has won major competitions throughout the country.

In a 2004 interview Vizier reflected on his career. "I was ahead of everybody. Everyone else was just starting. I was hard to beat...In 30 years of competition I've got cases and cases of ribbons. I don't know what I'd do if I couldn't compete. I've done some art. I've done some decorative stuff, but I'd rather do working decoys. To get it right takes quite a bit of effort. You have to put the wind in the bird." [Vizier, interview]

Right: Jimmie Vizier. "Canada Goose," 1990 (16 1/4" x 8 1/2" x 10 1/2")

Jimmie Vizier. "Wigeon Drake," 1990 (15 1/2" x 6" x 6 1/2")

Jimmie Vizier. "Pintail Drake," 1991 (20" x 6 1/4" x 7 3/4")

Larry Hayden (1934–)

Larry Hayden was born in Detroit, Michigan. Hayden's interest in art was encouraged by his mother, Helen, who was a fashion designer. After he graduated from St. Theresa High School in Detroit, he served an apprenticeship at the Professional Art Studio also in Detroit. From there he moved to the Triad Studios, where he considered his teachers of the highest quality. From 1957 to 1959 he was in the Army stationed in South Korea and working as an illustrator for the Army Newspaper.

By 1959 Hayden was a mature artist working at the Triad Studios in Detroit. During this time he studied under the painter Gordon McGowan. Hayden first became exposed to duck hunting in 1962. One of the salesmen working for the design studio took him out and he became fascinated with the sport. After this experience, he made eight mallard decoys for his own use. His experience with hunting ducks and making his own decoys led him to start participating in carving contests. At one of these he met the bird carver Jim Foote, who advised him early in his carving career to start studying birds if he wanted to be a good bird carver. He built a pen to keep live ducks to study. (Crandell, p. 3]

In 1971, he attended his first Ward Foundation World Championship Wildfowl Carving Competition in Salisbury, Maryland. He took with him four decorative decoys. All four won first place blue ribbons, a feat previously unheard of. One of these was the first completely wood-burned decoy, a wood duck drake. The drake pintail he entered won Best Marsh Duck and Best of Show. Over the years, Hayden entered thirteen more shows, and he won Best in Show every time. These shows included the U.S. National Show in New York, the Canadian National Show in Toronto, the Midwest Decoy Competition in Michigan, the International Decoy Show in Iowa, and again the Ward Foundation World Championship Wildfowl Carving Competition. Hayden was the first five-time Best of Show, Floating Decorative Decoy winner at the World Championship Wildfowl Carving Competition. Hayden very quickly became recognized as one of the most important bird carvers working in the last quarter of the twentieth century.

Left: Larry Hayden. "Wigeon Drake," 1973 (14 1/2" x 6" x 5 3/4")

His ideas about the way a decoy should be made influenced many of the decorative decoy makers working at that time and into the 21st century. He said, "The biggest flaw is in the unlikeness of the decoy to the species. The proportions are way off. Decoys have become so decorative that carvers are giving more attention to the intricacies of burning in feather detail and the paint job than they are to the basic carving. They wind up with something that just doesn't look like the real-life bird." [Crandell, p. 5] This was strong criticism from a bird carver who was noted for pioneering the use of high tech woodburning tools and grinders. But Hayden was noted for sharing his ideas with other carvers.

Bird carving was only one aspect of Larry Hayden's art. Making decoys was an expression of his love of nature and birds. By 1977 he started entering duck stamp competitions. He won ten duck stamp painting competitions from 1977 through 1995. He won the competition in Michigan three times. His attention to detail, which brought him so much recognition, was carried over into his paintings. World champion carver Jim Foote said that Hayden was responsible for moving the art form to a new level with his technical approach combined with the eye of the artist. [Carnaghi, p. 1]

Right: Larry Hayden. "Wood Duck Drake," 1974 (13 1/2" X 5 3/4" X 5 1/2")

Larry Hayden. "Scaup Drake," 1974 (14 1/2" X 7" X 8 1/4")

Larry Hayden. "Pintail Drake," 1974 (20" x 6 1/2" x 8 1/2")

Larry Hayden. "Bufflehead Pair," 1975 (drake:11 1/2 x5" x 6 1/2"; hen 10 1/2" x 5" x 10 1/2")

Larry Hayden. "Canvasback Hen," 1977 (13 1/4" x 6 1/2" x 6 1/2")

Larry Hayden. "Canvasback Drake," 1975 (14 3/4" x 7" x 8 1/2"

Larry Hayden. "Blue-winged Teal Pair," 1979 (drake: 11 3/4" x 4 3/4" x 5 1/4"; hen: 10 3/4" x 4 1/2" x 5 1/2")

LARRY

Left: Larry Hayden. "Canada Geese," 1992 (19 3/4" x 16")

Larry Hayden. "Blue-winged Teal" (19 3/4" x 16")

Larry Hayden. "Mallards," 1991. (19" x 14") This painting was used for the 1992 Texas Duck Stamp.

Larry Hayden. "Canvasbacks" (19 5/8" x 15 3/4")

Andrew "Tan" Brunet (1938–)

Another carver in the Cajun tradition, Tan Brunet was born in 1938, in Galliano, Louisiana. He was the youngest of five children. He estimates his family came to the United States from French Canada around the beginning of the 19th century. Louisiana has a rich history of decoy carving and the traditional aspects of the art form rubbed off on him. Brunet says he started carving at the age of ten. The Vizier family lived next door to him when he was growing up and Jimmie taught Tan how to carve. [Brunet, interview]

In the late 1960s, Dr. Harry Walsh of Easton, Maryland, invited Tan Brunet to attend the Easton Waterfowl Festival. From that time, Brunet and his family, including his two sons, champion carvers Jett and Jude, have traveled to Maryland twice a year to attend the Easton Waterfowl Festival and the Ward Foundation's World Championship Wildfowl Carving Competition. He very quickly learned that, with his talents, he could make a living as a decoy maker, establishing contacts with buyers at bird carving events and wildlife festivals. For many years he worked with his father Elphege, Sr., and brother Elphege, Jr., in the family lumber business. By the early 1980s, they sold the business and Brunet became a full-time decoy maker.

Throughout his career, Brunet has been an innovator. He developed new techniques both for carving and for presenting and organizing his pieces. By 1977, Brunet had developed his own way of woodburning. When he first started working with pyro techniques, he used ice picks heated on the kitchen stove. Though a rather primitive method of burning feathers, it certainly helped him achieve an understanding of the delicate relationship between heat and wood. He quickly graduated to more sophisticated electric tools. In the years to come, the concept of developing color through the use of heat rather than paints proved to be revolutionary. Not only was he able to create the earthy browns present in many waterfowl, but he could also obtain a feeling of softness that had never been achieved before.

Brunet also improved the ways decoys are weighted. Because of the traditional ties with the hunting decoy or "block," all decorative decoys, because they are floated in competitions, are required to work much the same way as traditional decoys. Instead of using a keel and weight placed on the bottom of the carving, however, Brunet came up with his own method of balancing the bird in the water. After carving the decorative decoy

Left: Tan Brunet. "Green-winged Teal," 1977 (11 3/4" x 5" x 4 3/4")

Tan Brunet. "Mallard Drake," 1992 (16" x 7" x 6 3/4")

from one block of wood, he saws the bottom half off. He bores holes in the inside bottom of his carving. Before he reassembles the top and bottom, he floats the bottom half of his carving while he pours hot lead into the holes he has drilled. When the carving floats just right, he knows he has added enough weight. With this method, the weights are internal and the bird can go from the water to the mantelpiece. In 1977 he won the Ward Foundation World Championship Wildfowl Carving Competition with a pair of pintails weighted in this manner. His use of coloring was one of the main factors contributing to his win. He continues to obtain the visual feeling of softness in his decoys that is so difficult to achieve when carving wood.

Brunet is proud of the fact that he is primarily a "hatchet man" and that he uses a minimum of modern tools in the construction of his decoys. Prior to carving a bird, he does a drawing of his subject, then draws the bird on a piece of wood. Brunet works from a solid piece of cypress root or tupelo gum. By working in this fashion, he avoids the problem of covering up the neck joint, as the head and body are carved from the same piece of wood.

Brunet learned that winning competitions took more than just carving an excellent decoy. He saw he also needed to control the way his carvings were displayed and thought that they should be telling a story about the decoy world or his world living on Bayou LaFourche. In 1981 he made the base an important part of the carving, controlling the placement of the birds and the way he wanted his audience to view them. The base became a prominent part of the sculpture, an important visual element as well as a compositional tool of the maker. Tan Brunet's bases are large, adding a sense of visual massiveness to his carvings. He makes

Tan Brunet. Bottom of "Wood Duck Hen," 1991. Brunet, like Lem Ward before him, writes poems on the bottom of many of his carvings.

them of Honduras mahogany, adding a decorative pattern of color and a platform for him to reflect aspects of his culture in the carving. He first did this in his 1981 World Champion Pair of canvasbacks. Another example of this is the canvasback drake he carved for the Garfinkles in 1986. He placed it on a base designed with a fully rigged miniature canvasback decoy. Inscribed on the decoy is "Rani Day Decoy Co." This is a clever play on words, using Rani Garfinkle's name. Brunet's model is taken, not from the bird carving world, but from the wildfowl painters. His miniature decoy is a three-dimensional remarque, bringing the focus back to the patrons for whom he made the carving.

Even though he lives in Louisiana, his regular travels to the Eastern Shore of Maryland at an early stage of his professional career led Brunet to become close with Lem Ward. Like Ward, Brunet writes poetry and messages on the bottoms of his decoys. He uses every available surface to deliver his message to the viewer, either for the purpose of communicating to the person who commissioned the piece or to give a greater sense of poetry to the bird he is presenting. On the bottom of a mallard drake he made for Sandy Garfinkle in 1993 he wrote "—MALLARD DRAKE— The Animal—His massive body, richness in colors & power he exerts in flight, commands the respect of everyone as the master of ducks. Collection of Sandy Garfinkle. By Tan Brunet 10-20-1993."

Tan Brunet considers himself a decoy maker and is very proud of the tradition. His bird carvings go a long way toward keeping this tradition alive and educating the 21st century viewer about a life style that goes back well over 150 years.

Tan Brunet. "Cinnamon Teal," 1982 (12 1/2" x 5 1/4" x 4 1/4")

Tan Brunet. "Goldeneye Drake," 1983 (12 1/2" x 5 1/4" x 4 1/2")

Ian Brunet. "Canvasback Drake," 1984 (14" x 7 1/8" x 7 1/4")

Tan Brunet "Canvasback Drake" with remarque, 1986 (13 1/2" x 7 1/2" x 7 1/2"). Brunet, like many painters of wildfowl who produced limited edition prints, made a remarque for some of his carvings.

Ian Brunet. "Scaup Hen," 1986 (11 3/4" x 6 1/4" x 8 1/2"). Brunet carved a miniature remarque of a Canada goose, originally carved by Lem Ward and used as the logo of the Ward Museum. He also added an oyster bucket remarque attached to the carving's keel as the decoy's anchor.

Tan Brunet. "Redhead Hen," 1987 (12 3/4" x 6 1/2" x 6 1/2")

Tan Brunet. "Black Duck," 1987 (16 3/4" x 7" x 6 1/2")

Tan Brunet. "Pintail Hen," 1988 (15 3/4" x 6 1/4" x 7")

Tan Brunet. "Bufflehead Drake," 1989 (10 3/4" x 5 1/4" x 5 1/2")

Tan Brunet. "Wigeon Pair," 1990 (drake: 14 1/4" x 6 1/2" x 5 1/2"; hen: 14" x 6 1/4" x 5 3/4")

Tan Brunet. "Wood Duck Pair," 1991 (drake: 13 3/4" x 6 1/2" x 5 1/2"; hen: 13" x 5 3/4" x 6 3/4")

Tan Brunet. "Pintail Drake," 1990 (30" x 6 1/2" x 9")

Tan Brunet. "Redhead Hen," 1983 (13" x 6 1/8" x 6")

Tan Brunet. "Mallard Drake," 1993 (15 3/4" x 7" x 7")

Ian Brunet: "Scaup Hen," 1985 (11 1/2" x 6" x 6 1/2")

Tan Brunet. "Trumpeter Swan," 3/4 size, 1992 (24" x 10 1/4" x 16 1/8")

John Gewerth (1943–)

Left: John Gewerth. " Blue-winged Teal Pair," 1987 (drake: 10 3/4" x 4 1/2" x 4 1/2"; hen: 10 1/2" x 4 1/2" x 3 1/2")

John Gewerth's family always fished and enjoyed the outdoors. He was eighteen when he started hunting waterfowl with his friend Jim O'Neill, who also got him interested in collecting decorative decoys in 1975. Gewerth loved his decorative decoys, but quickly learned they cost more than he could afford. This led him to carving. The first decorative decoy he carved was a ring neck duck in 1975, which he entered in the U.S. Nationals held in Babylon, New York. He received an honorable mention and continued to enter bird carving contests throughout the United States. By 1977 he was competing as a professional.

Gewerth is a self-trained artist, but bird carvers Larry Hayden, Randy Tull, and Pat Godin played a major roll in his development as a decorative bird carver.

John Gewerth never carved full-time. His primary occupation was in the container industry. When he retired in 2002, he was Production Planning Director for the United States Can Company in Lockport, Illinois.

Through 1985 he had a fairly stress-free job and was able to carve during his free time. He said, "It was when the Continental Can Company merged with the United States Can Company that my work environment changed." [Gewerth, interview] He stopped carving for competitions in 1987 because of the increased demands of his work. Up until that time, he won twelve Best of Show awards from various carving contests held around the United States.

Since 1987, he has made decorative decoys for reproduction for Ducks Unlimited, the conservation organization, where they are used in the group's marketing and fund-raising activities. He also does work for Big Sky Carvers, who make decoy reproductions.

He feels the most difficult part of carving is to capture the personality and the attitude of the bird. He spends a great deal of time in the field watching birds and studying bird skins and photographs. He finds he can easily accomplish the technical aspects of bird carving, that is, the basic carving and painting of a decorative decoy.

He has never relied on bird carving for his income. He says, "Because bird carving is so labor intensive, it is very difficult for a professional bird carver to make enough birds for an adequate income." [Gewerth, interview] He thinks this is why so many professional bird carvers have turned to teaching. "This has caused a lot of clones and people are copying their teachers' styles. It used to be that you could know who made what bird when you went to a contest. That is not possible any more. The bird carvings all look alike today. Teaching has stifled the individual style of the carver." He feels that because he is self-taught his carvings have a unique style. [Gewerth, interview]

Marcus Schultz (1948–)

Marc Shultz's father, Bill Schultz, was a world champion bird carver and, as a boy, Marc watched his father carve and paint. Marc says he was unaware of the lessons that were being imparted until years later. [Schultz, letter] At the age of 27, he was inspired to supplement the battered rig that his father had carved as a teenager. As he worked on the twelve ringneck decoys, he was surprised when friends started showing an interest in them. He gave them away as fast as he finished them. Soon, he was adding detail, such as feather groups, texture, and more intricate painting. He decided he'd try selling them for $150 a pair, a hen and a drake. It worked and soon he found himself coming home from his career as an iron worker, and carving during evenings and weekends. By August 1981, he was so swamped with commissions that he decided to take a year off and complete his orders. One year wasn't enough and carving became his new career.

Marc won the Ward Foundation World Championship Decorative Decoy Pairs in 1986 with his carving of a pair of cinnamon teal. He continued to win many ribbons and awards over the years and became a teacher to future generations of bird carvers.

He says his objectives for his work have changed over time. Originally he viewed his work as a demonstration of his skill, but now he tries to convey a sense of time and place in his work. He strives to share his enthusiasm for places to which he travels. "It's an elusive goal, one more easily achieved with painting than with carving," he admits. "It involves guess work as I wonder whether the clues and symbolism in the piece will be convincing to anyone. I've been taken completely by surprise by the emotional roller coaster that I find myself riding, one day wondering if I've made a single good decision all day, the next day reassured with the results of a new technique." [Schultz, letter]

Marc's creativity comes through in his championship work and he vows to continue carving as long as he feels there is more room to explore. He is among the fourth generation of carvers who almost seem to have inherited their artistic abilities, as his harlequin duck in the Garfinkle collection demonstrates.

Left: Marcus Schultz. "Harlequin Drake," 1981 (12 1/2" x 5 1/2" x 5")

Robert Guge (1952–)

Bob Guge's father, Roy, made decoys, and as he got better at the art, he started entering them in competitions. As a child, Guge was always interested in watching birds, but seeing his father make carvings with greater and greater detail sparked Bob's interest in carving. By the time he was twelve he had carved a few small birds. [Guge, interview]

Though his interest in carving continued, by 1973 Guge was employed as a house painter. That year he and his wife made a trip to Chincoteague, Virginia, where they visited the decoy carver, Delbert "Cigar" Daisey, and Guge became serious about carving birds. After wandering all over Chincoteague looking for Daisey, they finally found him sitting at a desk in his garage and carving a decoy. Guge thought to himself that was what he would like to do. From that time on, whenever he got a chance he would work at carving birds. He put in eight hours a day painting houses and went home and started carving. [Sanders, p. 36] Eventually, he stopped painting houses and continued carving and painting birds. Although Bob is self-taught, his father, Cigar Daisey, and Harold Haertel all played a role in influencing his carving. [Badger, p. 10]

Guge works from his home. A self-proclaimed family man, having an occupation that allows him to be with his family while he is working is an ideal situation for him. Ever since the mid-1980s he has also been teaching people how to carve birds. For him it is a good way to add to his income while continuing to practice his art and meet interesting people. His studio consists of two rooms in his basement. One room is used for painting and the other is used for carving. He uses jelutong wood and acrylics to make his birds. Like so many successful bird artists, he has studied birds extensively. The area of Ohio where he lives has large flocks of birds migrating through each year, giving him ample opportunity to study the live bird. He varies his carvings, placing emphasis upon different aspects of each bird. It is more critical to him to create a sculpture that captures the essence of the bird than to have an exact replica of a bird. When asked about anatomical accuracy versus creativity he replied, "I don't choose one over the other. Sometimes I'm more concerned with accuracy and other times more concerned with being expressive. Both are important, but neither has to be more important than the other. I consider myself an artist and I'm more concerned with the whole sculpture and not just the bird." [Badger, p 10]

Left: Robert Guge. "Piping Plover," 1986 (5 1/2" x 3" x 7 1/8")

Robert Guge. "Dunlin," 1986 (6 3/4" x 3" x 6 1/2")

Guge makes two types of sculpture. His "primitives" represent a very loose approach to sculpture. They have what he calls "a very folksy feel" about them. [Guge, interview] A good example of this is the piping plover he carved in 1976. His more formal sculpture is extremely realistic and detailed.

Guge's kestrel and redpoll are striking additions to the Garfinkle collection. The redpoll is a very important carving for him. He incorporated the making of this bird into one of his classes. Usually Guge will carve a featured bird during his workshop, teaching his students by example and ending up with the same bird as his students at the end of a class. Once he had started carving the redpoll, however, it became something more than a class example. After he finished it, he and his wife decided it was special enough that they were going to keep it for themselves. He brought it to the Ward Foundation's World Championship Wildfowl Carving Competition in the early 1990s and Sandy Garfinkle saw it and liked it. He wanted to buy it, but Guge didn't want to sell. Then Garfinkle offered him more for it than Guge would normally have asked for it, and Guge was impressed with the fact that Garfinkle liked it so much he was willing to pay a premium for it. He called his wife, Jody, and they agreed to sell the redpoll to Sandy Garfinkle. They had just bought a new house and were able to use the money for their new home. [Guge, interview]

Bob Guge has earned a reputation as one of the most important bird sculptors of the late 20th and early 21st centuries. He has won the Ward Foundation's World Championship Miniature category five times and is a top prize winner in most of the other major bird carving competitions held in the United States.

Robert Guge. "Kestrel," 1986 (6 1/2" x 17 1/2")

Robert Guge. "Redpoll," 1991 (8" x 5" x 21")

Robert Guge. "Redpoll,"
1991 (detail)

Patrick Godin (1953–)

Left: Patrick Godin. "Red-breasted Merganser Hen," 1980 (17 1/2" x 6 1/4" x 6 1/2")

Pat Godin began carving when he was eleven years old, carving fishing lures to use in Ontario, Canada, where he grew up. This early experience gave him a good grounding in using knives. When he was fourteen he read Eugene V. Connett's book, *Decoys: How to Make Them, How to Paint Them and How to Use Them*. At this time he was very intrigued with fooling ducks. Godin said, "I felt a fascination with the behavioral aspects of actually fooling a wild creature into thinking a painted block of wood was one of its own. So I went home and created a rather crude rendition of a preening black duck. My plans to make a whole rig were discouraged, however, when I discovered how much work was involved using the inappropriate tools I had. To add further insult to my pride the darned thing sank on its first test run. That was in 1968 and it wasn't until 1972 that I attempted such a project again." [Doerzbach, p. 4]

In 1970 he went to his first carving contest, the Canadian National Sportsmen's Show in Toronto, Canada. This was an important experience for him because it was at the "Nationals" that he was inspired by the work of bird carvers Jim Foote, Larry Hayden, William Schultz, John Garton, and John Scheeler. These bird carvers are recognized as some of the most important decoy makers in the history of contemporary bird carving. The influence of these artists, combined with his youthful love of the outdoors and nature, led him to dedicate his life to the study of animals and the environment.

His primary interest was always waterfowl. His early interest in waterfowl led him to assemble a sizable collection of mounted birds. These were his first lessons in ornithology. He very quickly learned about bird anatomy. While attending college at the University of Guelph, he continued to carve. In 1974, after making a rig of six decoys, he carved a goldeneye hen and entered it in the Canadian National Decoy Contest. It was judged runner-up for Best in Show. Next he won Best of Show Amateur in the World Championship Wildfowl Carving Competition in Salisbury, Maryland. He won the World Championship Decorative Decoy Pairs with a pair of goldeneye ducks in 1976.

Godin earned a B.S. in Fisheries and Wildlife Biology in 1976 and a M.S. in Waterfowl Ecology in 1979 from the University of Guelph. His masters thesis was "A Survey of Relationships between the Spatial and Temporal Distributions of Mallards and Pond Ecology in Southwestern Ontario." He spent a great deal of time observing how mallard distribution was related to the physical, chemical, and biological characteristics of wetlands. During his graduate work he also taught ornithology classes. Trained as an ornithologist and a scientist, he developed a thorough knowledge of birds that prepared him to become the recognized bird carver he is today.

Godin points out, “It will always remain impossible for me to segregate the logic and preciseness of science from the art in my work. It is very important to me that my pieces are biologically, anatomically, and ecologically correct. To accomplish this obviously requires much research. However, the big challenge is to incorporate the artistic components of aesthetically appealing composition in both form and color.” [Doerzbach, p. 5] His passion for birds and his growing interest in carving competitions led him to produce his first competition carvings. He would see the work of important carvers and go home and try to carve what he saw. He says, “The compositional aspects of art in general tend to dominate my train of thought when planning a piece. In fact, I have become so obsessed with this that I feel I must be in total control of every component in the composition. Nothing can be left to fate or accident. Every bend in a branch, every apparently random location of a leaf or a stone, every color scheme must be carefully planned.” [Doerzbach, p. 6]

There are a number of carvers in his generation who developed their own styles. Many taught themselves how to carve without the influence of a specific teacher. He taught himself the technical aspects of the art form and he emphasizes that he was influenced by many of the successful carvers who were working in the 1970s. To be successful he feels the artist needs to develop his own style, not someone else's. At a very early stage he realized he had to express some creativity in what he was doing. “It is important to me that I maintain a fresh and exciting quality in my work. I always remain open to new ideas and am willing to explore new directions in the art form of nature sculpture. I prefer to refer to my art as nature sculpture rather than bird sculpture or carving since I want to feel free to incorporate other components. For my art to be complete these other components must not only be accurate and realistic but also must be an important part of the composition.” [Doerzbach, p. 5]

He likes his carvings to tell stories and says that many of his pieces have some theme, expressing his interpretation of something going on in nature. He uses the bird as a vehicle to show aspects of nature. A grasshopper held in a black duck hen's mouth, for instance, places her in spring mating season when she requires a lot of protein for egg formation.

In the mid-1980s, Sandy Garfinkle had already acquired a common merganser hen made by Godin. By 1985, Pat Godin had won the World Champion Decorative Decoy Pairs three times. Garfinkle acquired a green wing teal made in 1988 and a blue wing teal made in 1989. Around this time Godin had already done a few fairly complex sculptures, and had been thinking

Right: Patrick Godin. “Oldsquaw Drake,” 1983 (17 1/2" x 6 1/4" x 6 1/4")

about doing a pintail pair for some time. He had been studying the work of bird sculptor Grainger McKoy and was very impressed with the dynamic tension this artist was able to create in his large environmental constructs. Godin wanted to create the same dynamics in his carvings of waterfowl that McKoy was able to produce in his works. [Godin, interview]

He spoke to Garfinkle about his ideas for making a pintail shaking his feathers, exploding with energy. Garfinkle agreed to support this project. Godin made the drake first. The patron liked it and commissioned a hen to go along with the drake. One of his main objectives was to make a pair of birds that complemented each other. He first made a clay model of both birds. This pair is the most complex floating waterfowl, in concept and execution, he has made. The pintail suits this style of carving because of its interesting feather shapes. The pair lends themselves to the development of very dramatic effects working with negative and positive space that creates a rhythm within each piece and between both pieces. Still working within the tradition of the decoy, showing the birds as if they were floating, the addition of ruffled feathers gives them an appearance of motion within space.

In the 1980s, Pat Godin married Jessica Vizier, daughter of Jimmie, one of the leading Cajun carvers from a long line of Louisiana decoy makers. The early influence of the Michigan decoy makers Jim Foote and Larry Hayden was brought together with the traditional decoy forms of Louisiana. Godin's abilities to synthesize regional stylistic trends and produce bird images that are unique have had a strong influence on the direction of the art form. Many carvers of the fourth generation cite Godin as an inspiration and spend hours talking with him.

Right: Patrick Godin. "Blue-winged Teal Drake," 1988 (11 1/2" x 4 1/2" x 5")

Patrick Godin. "Green-winged Teal Drake," 1989 (10 3/4" x 4 1/2" x 4 1/2")

Patrick Godin, "White-winged Scoter Drake," 1990 (15 1/2" x 6 3/4" x 5 3/4")

Patrick Godin. "Mallard Drake," 1989 (17" x 6 1/2" x 6 1/4")

Patrick Godin. "Pintail Pair," 1991 (drake:16 3/4" x 8 1/4" x 7 1/2"; hen: 13 1/2" x 8 1/4" 7 1/4")

Barbara Nelson (1955–)

Barbara Nelson. "Ruffed Grouse," 1991 (16" x 10" x 16 3/4")

Born and raised in the New England area, Nelson's career as a sculptor grew from her childhood fascination for wildlife and art. Those early interests led her to a B.S. degree in Wildlife Biology from the University of Massachusetts, followed by careers with the U.S. Forest Service, the U.S. Fish and Wildlife Service, and finally with the Iowa Department of Natural Resources. In 1989 she culminated her career in wildlife biology by receiving an appointment by the Governor of Iowa to the State Natural Resources Commission. In 1992 she was elected chairman of that commission.

During her years in Iowa, Nelson's avocation for art and her full-time activities in wildlife management merged into a new career in realistic bird carving. Local and regional recognition in competition came early and frequently. In 1989 her work was awarded world class recognition when she won the title of Second Best in World Lifesize with a ring necked pheasant titled "Sneak" in the Ward Foundation competition. At this point in the history of realistic bird carving an interpretive, more artistic presentation of the theme was evolving. It was not enough to simply carve a well executed bird. "Sneak" was noted by critics as displaying the unusual quality of combining a flawless, true-to-life pheasant on a contemporary, sickle-shaped black base with corn stalks carved in relief.

In 1991 Nelson repeated a world class win by capturing third in World Lifesize with a ruffed grouse. In this case, the grouse and the base were carved from one block of wood and had a decidedly Asian influence. Once again, there was an interpretation of the bird's habitat carved in relief on a stark, black background.

Upland game birds and waterfowl were naturally favorite themes for Nelson. Her work in wildlife management in the Prairie Pothole region of northwest Iowa gave her frequent, up-close contact with these animals. Many of Barbara's days in Iowa were spent hunting the wetlands, uplands, and woods for ducks, geese, pheasants, and grouse with her yellow Labrador retriever, Shar. Always a strong supporter of conservation organizations, Nelson served on the Board of Wetlands for Iowa and was the cofounder of the Ladies Chapter of Ducks Unlimited.

Soon after the win with the ruffed grouse Nelson's interest expanded to bronze sculpture and other themes. Eventually, Shar passed away and hunting was no longer important to Nelson, so she turned her talents to themes of horses and dogs, and the sports involving them. Her recent works in bronze include thoroughbred racing themes, fox hunting, life-size fox sculpture, and canine commissions. Nelson has created the United States Combined Training Hall of Fame Award, the Perpetual Trophy for the Madison Square Garden Grand Prix, and the South Carolina Huntsman's Perpetual Trophy. She is an experienced rider who enjoys fox hunting, show jumping, eventing, and golf.

Nelson is a member of the Society of Animal Artists. She has been the Master Carver for the Easton Waterfowl Festival and the featured sculptor for the Southeastern Wildlife Exposition. Although retired from competition, she still occasionally creates bird carvings. She and her husband now reside in Aiken, South Carolina, along with their dogs, cats, and horses. [Nelson, letter]

Michael Bonner (1956–)

Michael Bonner has been firmly rooted in the decoy tradition since he was born in Grand Rapids, Michigan. Coming from a family of artists and bird carvers, he started going to carving shows and contests when he was two years old. From an early age he was influenced by his father, Dick Bonner, who as a young boy had been inspired to carve birds by his father, a taxidermist and deer hide tanner. The decoy maker John Zackman and the Ward brothers' carvings were also early influences on his work, but his father was his main inspiration. The same could probably be said for Michael's brother Chris Bonner, who is also a noted decorative bird carver. [Bonner, interview]

In 1975, the family moved to New Orleans, Louisiana. Dick Bonner at that time was running a sporting goods store, though he eventually became a full-time bird carver. Bonner's mother was a wildlife and nature painter.

Michael Bonner carves mainly decorative decoys, which he started seriously carving in 1982, entering his carvings in traditional carving exhibitions, sportsmen's shows, and contests throughout the United States. He started going to the Ward Foundation World Championship Wildfowl Carving Competition held in Ocean City, Maryland, in 1984, winning in many categories.

Left: Michael Bonner. "Ring-necked Duck Pair," 1990 (drake: 10 3/4" x 6" x 6 3/4"; hen: 11" x 5 1/2" x 5 1/2")

Michael Bonner. "Shoveler Pair," 1990 (drake: 12 1/2" x 6 1/4" x 6"; hen: 13 1/2 x 6 1/2" x 4 1/2")

Michael Bonner. "Pintail Drake," 1990 (18 3/4" x 16 1/4" x 10")

In 1994 Bonner stopped entering contests. He says he would like to see the art form get away from competition. "Replicating a bird is not where it is," he believes. "We are in a transition period from events that were initially set up by the traditional hunter decoy maker who supported sporting shows and carving contests to more formal art exhibitions." He does not think bird carving competitions fully support the younger people who are taking up bird carving. He explains, "The contest today limits the creativity of the bird carver. Because of this everything tends to look the same." [Bonner, interview]

Since 1994, he has worked as a full-time carving instructor. Bonner uses tupelo gum and oil paint to make his decoys. He employs the traditional tools, a knife, hatchet, gouges and rasps, along with modern grinders and woodburning tools to make his birds.

Bonner makes three to four birds a year. He says, "I make what I see." If he sees something pretty, he makes it. His home is in the Bayou Savage National Wildlife Refuge where he does a great deal of bird watching. He likes "to pick a little piece of nature and capture it so that people don't have to walk out into a marsh to see it. I want to bring it into their homes." [Bonner, interview]

Right: Michael Bonner. "Canvasback Pair," 1991 (drake: 13 1/2" x 7 1/4" x 7 1/2"; hen: 13 1/2" x 7" x 7 1/4")

Larry Barth (1957–)

Larry Barth has always been interested in birds. His earliest childhood memories include bird watching. He was fourteen when he first started carving. He began making small bird charms for bracelets and selling them to a local florist for thirty-five cents. At that time he didn't know anyone else who was carving birds. His father did woodworking and he had easy access to any tools he might need. He continued making and selling small birds all through his high school years.

During the spring of his freshman year at Carnegie Mellon University's College of Fine Arts, he and his family made a visit to the Eastern Shore of Maryland. He noticed posters for the World Championship Wildfowl Carving Competition. He saw there were other people interested in making wooden birds. In the fall, they returned to Salisbury, Maryland, to visit the Ward Foundation's Wildfowl Carving and Art Exhibition. During the visit he realized that this was what he wanted to do for the rest of his life.

Though he was enrolled in the design program at Carnegie Mellon and ultimately took a degree in illustration, throughout his college years he continued to develop his skills as a bird carver. His independent studies included a wall-mounted carving of a great-horned owl and chicks, which he entered in the World Championship Lifesize Decorative Class. With his first entry, he won second place in the competition. The carving world was amazed at the skill and vision of this unknown young man. Since then he has gone on to win the World Championship eleven times.

"Algonquin" was the first carving for which he won a blue ribbon, in 1984. Though he had been carving for years by this time and had entered the World Champion class, he had not taken a first place in general competition prior to this. He found he could sell everything he could make.

The loons were a turning point in his personal artistic direction. He considered this a piece of sculpture as opposed to a bird carving. The concepts he used in making this piece solved a number of traditional visual problems. The piece is a presentation of two loons swimming. In order to do this he had to figure out how to make the water. To carve the water super realistically would not work. The water needed to be integrated into the whole carving. At this time many carvers created the sculptural image of water by using epoxy resins. For Barth this didn't work visually. He felt he needed to make the whole sculpture out of one piece of wood. For Barth, water is very difficult to portray. He explains "You are better off trying to find a way to artistically portray water than to make something that looks

Left: Larry Barth. "Algonquin," 1983 (14 1/2" x 9" x 4")

exactly like water. To go at water directly is not the most effective way to do it. It is more important to create the impression of water." [Barth, interview]

The loons work best with backlighting. It is the shape and form that are important, not the detail. He wants the viewer to be caught up in the mood of the piece, not in the minutia. This is not a portrait of loons; it is a Canadian lake that has loons on it. He feels that if he had made the piece life-size the focus would be on the birds. When it is backlit the plumage of loons doesn't matter to the viewer, but the shape does. The water sparkles and you are seeing not the water, but the light on the water. This was a pivotal piece for his development as an artist. His aim is not to make bird carvings but to make sculptures dealing with all of the visual problems artists traditionally have had: form, spatial organization, negative and positive space, mass and transparency.

The "Black Throated Green Warbler" and the "Black and White Warbler" are also considered pivotal pieces for Larry Barth. In the mid 1980s, John Scheeler, Eldridge Arnold, and Larry Barth all started making black boxes for their bases. Arnold's blocks were low and fat, Scheeler's were square cubes and Barth's were high rectangles. One of the reasons Barth started exploring black rectangles for his bases was that he was becoming disillusioned with the way work was presented at exhibitions and contests. At this time, the events would pack hundreds of carvings together on tables in large halls. He felt his work was more important than this, and that it was not the way to display art.

Since the work would not be placed on a stand but clustered with many other carvings made by other people, he decided to incorporate the display pedestal into the work itself. He explains, "This made the piece look clean and contemporary and traditional at the same time." [Barth, interview] He was always intrigued with the realization that sometimes the best way to hide something is to be blatant about it. He feels the black box is so obvious it becomes invisible. To him the image of the bird is more important.

"The Warblers," which look very simple, were very complex in conception. In the early 1980s bird carvers were more concerned with very intricate compositions and used a great amount of detail in their work. Barth found that going in the opposite direction, minimizing the materials and the presentation of the sculpture, was an important part of accomplishing his goal of capturing the essence of his subject. In many ways he was working on some of the same problems the Romanian sculptor, Constantin Brancusi, faced in his "Bird in Space" series.

Right: Larry Barth. "Black-throated Green Warbler" (9" x 8" x 19 3/4") and "Black-and-white Warbler" (8" x 7" x 21 1/2"), 1986

Barth feels that proportions of settings are important. He explains, "To put a little bird on a small branch makes the bird look larger than it should. To place it on a large branch makes the bird look small." [Barth, interview] Though simple in concept, this is an important visual understanding that has affected much of Barth's work since "The Warblers."

He finds magical and surprising visual effects can be achieved by pushing proportions to extremes. A lot of this has to do with the expectations of the viewer. "When they are expecting mass, give them line. When they are expecting color, give them pattern instead. By coming up with the unexpected you achieve a stronger visual and intellectual impact." [Barth, interview]

The "Saw Whet Owl" is a fuller realization of the visual problem solving that Barth began exploring with "The Warblers," and a culmination of his exploration into simplification and organization. This piece is important to him because of the way he is now using metal in his sculptures. He started using a welding torch to fabricate parts of his sculptures in 1987. The making of the white pine in this piece would have been impossible without using welded metal. He points out, "Pre-visualization is important to the full realization of the work of art. All components of a sculpture should fall into place prior to starting a piece." [Barth, interview] The use of metal in his work facilitates his ability to realize what he sees in his imagination. This is now typical of the work that comes out of his shop. He finds himself increasingly using metal.

With all of his pieces, the use of negative and positive space is key. He likes the piece to take up more "visual space" than the actual "physical space" it fills. To do this, he feels the artist needs to contemplate the space around the piece. He has achieved this with all of his work since "The Warblers." His art training and willingness to experiment continue to raise the bar in the carving world.

Right: Larry Barth. "Black-throated Green Warbler," 1986 (detail)

Left: Larry Barth. "Black-and-white Warbler," 1986 (detail)

Right: Larry Barth. "Saw-whet Owl," 1990 (26" x 13" x 10")

Rick Johannsen (1958–)

Like many successful bird carvers, Rick Johannsen started carving miniature ducks at an early age. His first miniature decoys were carved along side his father and brothers, all of whom are duck hunters. All his life he has been exposed to the making and use of decoys as part of the waterfowling tradition, which is very strong in northern Ohio. He says that, "Each miniature I made I tried to make it fancier than the previous one I had made." [Johannsen, interview]

In the early 1970s, at the age of seventeen, he attended a wildfowl carving exhibition sponsored by the Ohio Decoy Carvers and Collectors Association. He was fascinated by the high level of skill and creativity expressed in the carvings that were on display at this event. It was at this event that he first met bird carver Robert Franta and was very taken with his work. He wanted to obtain the same level of realism that Franta was able to achieve.

Over the years Johannsen continued to make decoys, always striving to make a better bird with each carving he completed. In 1980, his friend Dick Gordy asked Johannsen if he would teach him how to carve decoys. The two began carving birds together. In 1984 Gordy told Johannsen that Robert Franta was going to be teaching a decorative bird carving class in the area where they lived. They took Franta's class, where Johannsen carved a drake canvasback. After taking this course he entered his next carving at the Ward Foundation's World Championship Wildfowl Carving Competition and won his first blue ribbon. He says he was hooked and he's been carving ever since. In 1988, he won Best of Show Intermediate Class. In 1991, he won Best of Show with a hen pintail that the Garfinkles purchased for their collection.

When Rick was not carving birds, he was farming about 1300 acres with his father and brother. But with the increase in development and the cost of farming he switched jobs, acting as the manager for a private hunting club and, during the slower winter months, carving birds.

In 2003, he won the World Championship Shootin' Rig competition with a rig of three redheads. He feels that over the years his work has continued to get better. He recognizes that the business of bird carving has changed, and it seems to him that there are fewer bird carvers than there were in the 1980s. Still, Rick is solidly involved in the hunting tradition that spawned this art form over 150 years ago. Because he guides hunters and uses decoys, his work reflects its original purpose.

Left: Rick Johannsen. "Pintail Hen," 1991 (13 1/2" x 6 1/2" x 6 1/2")

Greg Woodard (1958–)

Greg Woodard was born in Prescott, Arizona. His mother used to tell him he was "...born under a cactus." [Woodard, letter] Greg says he has always felt that he belonged outdoors. His father had a tremendous love of nature and enjoyed watching and identifying birds. The bird books Greg received for Christmas remain some of his most prized possessions. Once, on a family vacation, Greg saw a bird carving in a gift shop and wondered if people made a living doing that kind of work, thinking it would be a good career for him.

After high school, he worked with his father in a cabinet shop and carved decoys on the side. His first decoy was carved using only a duck stamp print for reference. Today he believes proper referencing and a thorough knowledge of the subject includes study skins, measurements, and studies of live birds and photographs. He believes one should also have an understanding of the bird's environment and habits.

He began to attend art festivals and joined a local carving club, where he was influenced by champion carver, Lance Turner. Turner encouraged him to enter competitions and offered constructive criticism. Greg entered a spoonbill hen in a 1985 Sacramento, California, show in the Novice Class. Just as he walked into his hotel room after delivering the bird, the phone rang. It was Art Bond, a San Francisco gallery owner, asking him if he had an agent. Bond tried to get Greg's piece out of the Novice Division to increase its value, but was not successful. Greg took Best in Show in his class and started a relationship with Bond.

Left: Greg Woodard. "Peregrine Falcon," 1987 (10" x 9" x 28")

Greg says he "...lived in the cabinet shop, ate tuna sandwiches, and lived for carving birds." [Woodard, letter]

His next show was in 1986 in San Diego, California, where he entered his first raptor, a peregrine falcon with its prey, an avocet. This time he entered the Open Class and placed in the top three. At the 1987 Ward Foundation World Championship Wildfowl Carving Competition in Ocean City, Maryland, he entered and received an honorable mention. The next year he came back with a peregrine falcon standing on a rock which placed in the top three in its class. The following year he returned with a peregrine falcon with a spread tail and took Best in Show in its class. He continued to win various prizes across the country, including five Best in Show ribbons from the Ward competition. In 1992, he won the Ward World Championship Decorative Lifesize and the following year won the Ward World Championship Interpretive prize.

Mostly self-taught, he is a master falconer and raptor breeder, and this familiarity with birds of prey makes them his favorite subjects. Experimentation, growth, and experience move him forward. Recently he has been working with bronze sculpture and painting it for effect.

Right: Greg Woodard. "Peregrine Falcon," 1995 (10" x 7" x 18 3/8")

Left: Greg Woodard. "Peregrine Falcon," 1995, back view.

Right: Greg Woodard. "Gyrfalcon," 1996 (11" x 11" x 29 1/2")

Gary Yoder (1958–)

Step back into the eighteenth century and into Gary Yoder's log cabin workshop. Tucked into the hills of Garrett County, Maryland, Yoder works among several eighteenth century cabins which make up the Penn Alps, an artisans' community. It is this village of transplanted cabins which gave him his start in the carving world. Over thirty years ago, Dr. Alta Shrock, a university professor, conceived a village where artisans could work and visitors could watch them create. Yoder decided to try a class at Penn Alps, and from offerings in basket making, pottery, and wood carving, he chose carving. He was told to bring a sharp pocketknife. The potter working in the village also whittled and showed Yoder the basics. Before long, Yoder was the resident carver – at the young age of thirteen – and he has been working at Penn Alps ever since. He enjoys talking to people about his work, but uses the long, snowy winters to do most of his serious carving.

It was natural for Yoder to carve birds. He says he has always had a passion for birds and is a "birdwatcher first and a carver second." [Yoder, interview] Isolated way out in western Maryland, he carved the songbirds he saw around him and didn't think about ducks or decoys. A friend told him about the Ward carving contest, and he decided to enter in 1973 at the age of fourteen. He says the double doors of the exhibit hall opened to frame John Scheeler's upright falcon clutching a dead green-winged teal. "There could have been music. I knew I wanted to carve like that." [Yoder, interview] It was one of many inspirational moments for him, and he returned year after year, more for the camaraderie than for the challenge.

Left: Gary Yoder. "Tricolored Heron," 1991 (14" x 11 1/2" x 24")

His first year he hardly spoke to anyone, but now he cherishes the conversations with Pat Godin, Bob Guge, and Larry Barth. He was inspired by Scheeler and the carvers of Scheeler's generation, like Jim Foote. Once he was having trouble blending acrylics and he asked Foote for advice. Jim simply answered, "Change your technique." [Yoder, interview] To Yoder, this kind of interaction is the strength of the contests and his reason for going. Yoder continues to compete and has won five World Championships, four in the Miniature and one in the Lifesize categories. Best known for his fine miniatures, the carving of the Louisiana heron in the Garfinkle collection is his largest full-size piece.

He says the nature of wood, being subtractive, doesn't allow for mistakes, so he often works up a clay model for his composition and design. He sketches his ideas, visits banding stations, and uses anything he can find to help provide the details of his work. He reiterates that the dialogue with other carvers at shows is very important in acquiring technique and getting feedback. He recalls when Lem Ward picked up one of his simplest early carvings and said, "Keep carving." He is.

Right: Gary Yoder. Detail of "Tricolored Heron," 1991 (detail)

Jett Brunet (1964–)

Around 1972, Jett Brunet was watching his father, Tan, carve decoys in the family's kitchen, when the seven-year-old realized he was going to be a sculptor of birds. Plastic had taken over the market for hunting decoys, so Jett's father was actively making the transition from hunting decoys to decorative decoys. Jett Brunet watched his father create his birds. He also saw his father developing the techniques necessary to make a decorative decoy. While steeped in the traditions of decoy making, Tan still used a hatchet, spoke shave, and rasp, but he needed to develop techniques and skills for the fine work of carving every hair in the bird's feathers.

Jett was impressed with the way Tan was able to solve technical problems on his own without having any formal instruction in sculpture or carving. This was probably one of the most important early lessons he was to learn from his father. He knew that he, too, could become a sculptor. Since 1971, the whole Brunet family had been traveling to the Eastern Shore of Maryland to participate in the Easton Waterfowl Festival and the Ward Foundation World Championship Wildfowl Carving Competition, so even as a young child, Jett had experienced the excitement that was generated by the gathering of people from all over the United States and Canada who made wooden birds. It was natural for this young boy to also want to become part of this creative group.

Jett Brunet followed in his father's footsteps. His first and only teacher was Tan Brunet. He started carving at the age of nine and began competing for ribbons and purses at various contests and levels. His father stopped competing when Jett began entering the professional categories of the competitions. Jett won his first World Championship Decorative Decoy Pairs in 1985 with a pair of ruddy ducks. He was 21 years old at the time. [Brunet, interview]

Jett first met Sandy Garfinkle in 1986. He was a mature artist working full-time as a bird sculptor when Garfinkle first approached him to commission a carving of a cinnamon teal. Garfinkle actively collected Jett Brunet's work for about eight years. During this time he developed a close relationship with the Brunet family.

Sandy Garfinkle became a patron of Jett Brunet during a very important period of growth for the artist. Jett Brunet feels that the birds that Garfinkle acquired, as a whole, show his development from making decorative decoys to life-size bird sculpture. After winning the World Championship Decoy Pairs twice, Jett began looking in other directions. Sandy Garfinkle encouraged Brunet to start exploring the potential of his creative, intellectual, and technical skills. Brunet feels this encouragement led to the creation of his red-tailed hawk in 1988.

Left: Jett Brunet. "Wigeon Pair," 1984 (drake: 13 1/2" x 6 3/4" x 6 1/4"; hen: 12" x 6 1/2" 5 1/2)

Jett explained, "Larry Hayden and Tan Brunet had a great influence on the development of my style as a decoy maker. But it was John Scheeler who influenced me to try to make a bird of prey." [Brunet, interview] Both Scheeler and Hayden were two of the most important bird carvers working at the time Jett was making his name, but ultimately it was Garfinkle's encouragement and John Scheeler's work that influenced him to make the red-tailed hawk.

In 1990, the organizers of The Easton Waterfowl Festival in Easton, Maryland, asked Jett to make a bird carving that would be the featured work of art at the festival. The Easton area has a rich tradition of sport hunting for waterfowl. Because of the large numbers of hunters who descended upon the town in the fall of each year, in 1968 a group of residents, guides, and sportspeople thought it would be a good idea to have a festival that featured the great waterfowling traditions of the Eastern Shore of Maryland. The proceeds from this activity would be used for the conservation of waterfowl habitat. This event became an important venue for bird artists throughout the United States. To be asked to provide the featured work of art at the Easton Waterfowl Festival said to potential patrons that this was an important artist and would lead to increased commissions for the artist. Garfinkle encouraged him to take on this ambitious project and commissioned him to make the eagle. It was finished in 1991 and remains one of the most impressive pieces in the Garfinkle collection.

Jett Brunet continued to enter his works in bird carving contests around the country. Over a period of about five years he won over 35 Best of Show awards. He became recognized as one of the most important and innovative artists working in the area of wildfowl sculpture. By 1993 he began moving in two new directions. He started experimenting with the floating duck and, fascinated with the work of John Sharp and Leo Osburn, he started thinking about the bird as pure sculpture. Once again, with Garfinkle's encouragement, Jett produced a unique pair of mallards that he feels are two of the most important decorative decoys he has produced. [Brunet, interview]

Jett Brunet continues to carve decorative decoys, but increasingly his work is becoming more interpretative and much more in line with traditional sculpture, often leaving the birds unpainted with the visual emphasis upon form and structure. He seems to be using the bird more as a vehicle for visual ideas that do not necessarily have to do with the bird itself. The Cajun tradition, combined with his continual experimentation, continue to win Jett prizes and praise.

Right: Jett Brunet. "Redhead Drake," 1987 (12 1/2" x 6 1/2" x 7")

Jett Brunet. "Scaup Drake," 1987 (12 3/4" x 6 1/2" x 6 1/4")

Jett Brunet. "Pintail Drake," 1988 (18" x 7" x 7")

Jett Brunet. "Ruddy Duck Pair," 1990 (drake: 10" x 5 3/4" x 5 1/2"; hen: 10" x 5 1/4" x 5")

Jett Brunet. "Mallard Pair," 1992 (drake: 14" x 8 1/2" x 7"; hen: 12 1/2" x 7 1/2" x 7 1/4")

Jett Brunet. "Red-tailed Hawk," 1988 (21" x 19" x 20")

Jett Brunet. "Canvasback Drake," 1988 (14" x 7" x 8")

Jett Brunet. "Bald Eagle," 1991 (20" x 18" x 35")

Jett Brunet. "Black Duck Drake," 1990 (16" x 7" x 6")

Jude Brunet (1969–)

Being part of one of the most successful, if not the most important, families of contemporary bird carvers, it is surprising that Jude Brunet did not think of being a decorative decoy maker until he was twenty. Jude's father, Tan, and brother, Jett, had both won the coveted Ward Foundation World Championship Wildfowl Carving Competition held in Salisbury, Maryland, numerous times. Jude had watched his father and brother making birds all of his life. He also was artistically inclined. He graduated from the Art Institute of Houston in 1989 with a degree in commercial art. It was during his senior year in college that people started asking him to make decorative decoys for them. At first, he was not too interested in making decoys to order, but he found he seemed to have inherited the ability, and by the time he graduated he had four orders for carved birds.

He estimates he makes three or four decorative decoys in a year. He also enjoys making hunting decoys. Like his father and brother, he uses the traditional tools, hatchets, rasps, and spoke shaves, along with woodburning tools and grinders to make his decoys. When he talks about making his birds, he emphasizes that he uses acrylics for painting his hunting decoys and oil paint for his decorative decoys. Like his father, Tan, he talks about achieving a quality of softness in his carvings, referring to the quality of visual softness in the feathers, so soft the viewer wants to touch them. Jude feels he is a better painter than a

Jude Brunet. "Shoveler Drake," 1990
(13" x 6 1/4" x 6")

carver, though he has developed a unique style of carving. He is a very realistic painter, paying a great deal of attention to detail.

Like all bird carvers he studies birds all of the time. He is with his brother and father three to four days a week. He feels very fortunate to have such a supportive family and to be able to be with such knowledgeable, talented people. [Brunet, interview]

Jude Brunet has won the Ward Foundation World Championship Wildfowl Carving Competition, Decorative Decoy Pairs, twice. When asked why he entered this very competitive event he explained, "Because my brother and father both won it."

When he first started making decoys, he traveled to carving exhibitions and contests all over the United States. But in more recent years he has limited his travels to The Easton Waterfowl Festival in Easton, Maryland, in the fall, the Ward Foundation World Championship in Ocean City, Maryland, in the spring, and the Louisiana Wildfowl Carvers and Collectors Guild Wildfowl Festival in New Orleans, Louisiana. From his participation in these events he generates three or four commissions for decoys each year.

Ensconced in the hunting and carving tradition, it's almost as if the art chose him, rather than the other way around and his fine work is very collectible. His art training sets him apart from many of the other Cajun carvers.

Right: Jude Brunet. "Wigeon Drake," 1993 (14 3/4" x 6 3/4" x 6 1/2")

Todd Wohlt (1970–)

It is interesting that many of the bird carvers that make up the Garfinkle collection started as young people who, for the most part, taught themselves how to carve and paint. Todd Wohlt was twelve years old and his grandfather had passed away. His grandfather had been a professional duck hunting guide and a fisherman, and he left behind a rig of hunting decoys he had made and used over the years. The rig was pretty beat up, but when Wohlt saw the decoys he decided he was going to fix them up. Many of the heads were broken, and the bodies had been banged around from heavy usage, but he went to work fixing up his grandfather's decoys. His father finally told him not to do any more work on the gunning decoys because it would lessen the value of the decoys. [Sanders, p. 29]

Wohlt turned to carving miniature ducks, and continued carving his miniature decoys until 1984, when he visited the Leigh Yawkee Woodson Art Museum's annual "Birds in Art" exhibition. This exhibition, held at the museum in Wasaw, Wisconsin, showcases important contemporary working bird artists. While visiting the "Birds in Art" exhibit, he realized he wanted to become a bird carver. [Wohlt, interview]

In 1985, he entered a mallard drake in the Mid-Atlantic Wildfowl Festival held annually at Virginia Beach. He took third in the novice category. Marc Schultz won Best of Show with a wigeon, and John Scheeler suggested to Wohlt that he might want to take a class from Schultz, because he lived nearby. [Sanders, p. 29] A few weeks later Wohlt heard Schultz give a lecture on carving. He then enrolled in his class.

Wohlt felt this was an important experience for him and says he learned a great deal from Schultz. The most important lesson was to make his birds his own way. The next year, when he was 16 years old, he entered a wood duck in the novice category in the A. Danner Frazer competition for young people under the age of 18. This award is designed to encourage promising young people to make bird carvings. At the Ward Foundation competition he won both the A. Danner Frazer Award and Best of Show Novice Carver. He was still in high school at the time, and this experience confirmed his decision to be a bird carver.

Left: Todd Wohlt. "Pintail Hen," 1987
(15 1/4" x 5 1/4" x 5 1/2")

In 1987, Wohlt entered the University of Wisconsin at Stevens Point studying art. His father was an art teacher and he found himself going in the same direction. He continued making birds throughout his time at the university. In 1991, when he was in his last year at the university, Wohlt won his first World Championship Decorative Lifesize competition. He won it again in 2004.

Even though he has won the World Championship twice he does not work as a bird artist full-time. He presently works as an illustrator for a packaging company. He only makes one or two carvings a year. [Wohlt, interview] Wohlt works in the basement of his home. He is not able to make large birds or sculptures because of the size of the space he works in. Most of what he makes are miniature bird carvings and song birds because it is easier for him to manage these sculptures in small spaces. He says he likes trying to make wood look like feathers, to appear as something it is not. He uses any wood working tools that can do the various tasks necessary for making a carving. These include woodburning tools, chisels, knives, and grinders. Wohlt points out that he started out making ducks, but now does decorative bird carvings. He gets most of his ideas for his sculptures from wildlife painters and other bird carvers. In addition to Marc Schultz, he feels that Larry Barth, Ernie Muehlmatt, Pat Godin, and John Sharp have influenced his work. [Wohlt, interview]

He does whatever inspires him. He thinks carving competitions are good for the art form of bird carving. They help set a certain level of quality. "Carving competitions have their niche," he explained. [Wohlt, interview] Carving contests and exhibitions help give him ideas. Wohlt represents a new generation of carvers carrying on a tradition of working three-dimensionally.

Bibliography

Badger, Curtis. "The Brunets of Galliano," *Wildfowl Art, Journal of the Ward Foundation*. Salisbury, Maryland: Ward Foundation, Winter 1993, pp. 26-30.

Badger, Curtis. *Carving & Painting a Pintail Drake with Jimmie Vizier*. Mechanicsburg, Pennsylvania: Stackpole Books, 1999.

Badger, Curtis. "Bob Guge – A Reverence for Birds," *Wildfowl Art Journal of the Ward Foundation*. Salisbury, Maryland: Ward Foundation, Fall 1987, p. 10.

Barber, Joel. *Wildfowl Decoys*. New York: Dover Press, 1954, p. 9.

Barth, Larry. Personal interview with Kenneth Basile, 25 April 2005.

Basile, Kenneth. *American Decorative Bird Carving*. Salisbury, Maryland: Ward Foundation, 1981.

_____. "Champion Tan Brunet," *Wildfowl Art, Journal of the Ward Foundation*. Salisbury, Maryland: Ward Foundation, Fall 1982, pp. 4-7.

Birchler, Bob. "Rebirth of the 'Nationals,'" *Decoy Collectors Guide*, April/June, 1963, pp. 7-8.

Bonner, Michael. Personal interview with Kenneth Basile, 18 August, 2005.

Brunet, Jett. Personal interview with Kenneth Basile, 25 April, 2005.

Brunet, Jude. Personal interview with Kenneth Basile, 10 August, 2005.

Brunet, Tan. Personal interview with Kenneth Basile, May 2004.

Carnaghi, Leonard. Letter to Kenneth Basile, May 2005

Conner, Charles. *Louisiana Lures and Legends*. Golden Meadow, Louisiana: REM Corp., 1997, pp. 76-97.

Crandell, Bernard W. "Larry Hayden – A Living Legend," *North American Decoys*. Spanish Fork, Utah: Hillcrest Publications, Fall/Winter 1982, pp. 2-9.

_____. "Jim Foote – A Change of Pace," *North American Decoys*. Spanish Fork, Utah: Hillcrest Publications, Fall/Winter 1981, p. 2.

Doerzbach, Cindy. "Gary Yoder, Champion Miniature Carver," *Ward Foundation News*. Salisbury, Maryland: Ward Foundation, Fall 1982, pp. 8-11.

_____. "Pat Godin 1982 World Champion," *Ward Foundation News*. Salisbury, Maryland: Ward Foundation, Winter, 1982, pp. 4-7.

Foote, Jo Anne. Personal interview with Kenneth Basile, July 2005.

Freshour, John. Personal interview with Kenneth Basile, Centennial Office of The Smithsonian Institution, November 1978.

Gewerth, John. Personal interview with Kenneth Basile, 23 August 2005.

Godin, Pat. Personal interview with Kenneth Basile, 25 April 2005.

Guge, Bob. Personal interview with Lora Bottinelli, 25 April 2005.

Johannsen, Rick. Personal interview with Kenneth Basile, July 2005.

"Larry Barth's Owls," *North American Decoys*. Spanish Fork, Utah: Hillcrest Publications, Spring/summer, 1981, pp. 58-60.

Loeff, Ralph M. "Judging the Decorative Waterfowl Class," *Decoy Collector's Guide*. Burlington, Iowa: Harold Sorensen, 1965, pp. 10-11.

Mackey, William J., Jr. "The Life and Times of a Decoy Judge," *Decoy Collectors Guide*. Burlington, Iowa: Harold Sorensen, Vol. III, 1965, p. 9.

Muehlmatt. Ernest. Personal interview with Kenneth Basile, March 2005.

Nelson, Barbara. Letter to Kenneth Basile, 6 August 2005.

"Novel Decoy Exhibit Held at Bellport," *Patchogue Long Island Advance*, 30 August 1923.

Sanders, Donna. "More Small than Big," *Wildfowl Carving and Collecting*. Harrisburg, Pennsylvania: Stackpole Books, Winter 1988, p. 36.

_____. "Carving Out a Home Based Life-Style," *Wildfowl Art Journal of the Ward Foundation*. Salisbury, Maryland: Ward Foundation, Winter 1992, p. 7.

_____. "Todd Wohlt," *Wildfowl Carving and Collecting*. Harrisburg, Pennsylvania: Stackpole Books, Winter 1991, p. 29]

Schroeder, Roger. *John Scheeler Bird Carver*. Harrisburg, Pennsylvania: Stackpole Books, 1988.

Sorensen, Harold. "Bob Kerr – Canadian Carver," *Decoy Collector's Guide*. Burlington, Iowa: Harold Sorensen, Vol. III, 1965, p. 26]

_____. "Results of the Decoy Contest at Toronto," *Decoy Collector's Guide*. Burlington, Iowa: Harold Sorensen, Vol. III, 1965, p. 10.

_____. "Second American Bird Carving Exhibit Held at Chestertown," *Decoy Collector's Guide*. Burlington, Iowa: Harold Sorensen, 1968 Annual, p. 125.

Vizier, Jimmie. Personal interview with Lora Bottinelli, 24 April 2004.

Ward, Lemuel. Personal interview with Kenneth Basile, April 1981.

Witsul, Frank. "James Foote," *Detroit Free Press*, 16 August, 2004, p. 1.

Wohlt, Todd. Personal Interview with Lora Bottinelli, 24 April 2004.

Woodard, Greg. Letter to Kenneth Basile, June 2005.

Yoder, Gary. Personal interview with Kenneth and Karen Basile, 17 August 2005.

Acknowledgments

The Board of Directors and the staff of the Ward Museum of Wildfowl Art, Salisbury University are very grateful to the Garfinkles for their generosity. Our thanks go out to Sandy and Rani Garfinkle, Suzy Garfinkle Chevrier, and Steven and Victoria Garfinkle.

I also want to thank the Board of Directors of the Ward Foundation and the administration of Salisbury University for the encouragement they have given me to become involved in projects like this. All of the living artists whose works are in the Garfinkle Family Collection worked closely with me. I appreciate their support. Larry Barth, Jett Brunet, Rani Garfinkle, and Steven Garfinkle assisted me in preparing the collection, and they continued to advise me throughout this project. This project would not have happened without the work, support, and encouragement of Rani and Steven Garfinkle. Thanks go to Sam Dyke and Jo Ann Wilber who gave their time and advice for the development of this catalogue and the exhibition of the Garfinkle Family Collection. The Ward Museum/Garfinkle Family and Thirtieth Anniversary Reception Committee, chaired by Phil Adkins, gave generously of their time and skills. We couldn't have pulled this event together without them. The staff of the Ward Museum, as always, worked diligently with me throughout this project. I'm grateful to them for all of their help and enthusiasm for everything the Museum does. Deputy Director Lora Bottinelli managed to find time during the demands of the spring competition to help me with the important interview process for this catalogue. My wife, Karen Basile, spent many hours editing the catalogue and had many conversations with me to help define the format. I've been very fortunate; she has always been with me in every project I've taken on.

Kenneth Basile
Salisbury, Maryland

Carvings Illustrated

The Garfinkle Family, August 2003. Left to right: Rani Garfinkle, Sandy Garfinkle, Joelle Chevrier, Rebecca Garfinkle, Claire Chevrier, Sophi Garfinkle, Suzy Garfinkle Chevrier, Natalie Chevrier, Ari Garfinkle, Steven Garfinkle, Jakob Garfinkle, Victoria Garfinkle, Sue Garfinkle; Ben Garfinkle, Matthew Garfinkle (not pictured)

US $49.95
9 780764 325014 54995
ISBN: 0-7643-2501-9